TIME AND ETERNITY

TIME AND ETERNITY

Uncollected Writings 1933 – 1983

Malcolm Muggeridge

Foreword by Mother Teresa

Edited with an Introduction by Nicholas Flynn

ORBIS BOOKS

Maryknoll, New York 10545

Founded in 1970, Orbis Books endeavors to publish works that enlighten the mind, nourish the spirit, and challenge the conscience. The publishing arm of the Maryknoll Fathers and Brothers, Orbis seeks to explore the global dimensions of the Christian faith and mission, to invite dialogue with diverse cultures and religious traditions, and to serve the cause of reconciliation and peace. The books published reflect the views of their authors and do not represent the official position of the Maryknoll Society. To learn more about Maryknoll and Orbis Books, please visit our website at www.maryknollsociety.org.

First published in Great Britain in 2010 by
Darton, Longman and Todd Ltd
1 Spencer Court
140-142 Wandsworth High Street
London SW18 4JJ

First published in the USA in 2011 by
Orbis Books
P.O. Box 302
Maryknoll, New York 10545-0302

Library of Congress Cataloging-in-Publication Data

Muggeridge, Malcolm, 1903-1990.
Time and eternity : uncollected writings, 1933-1983 / Malcolm Muggeridge; foreword by Mother Teresa; edited with an introduction by Nicholas Flynn.
       p. cm.
  Includes bibliographical references (p.   ).
  ISBN 978-1-57075-905-5 (pbk.)
  I. Flynn, Nicholas. II. Title.
  PR6025.U5T56 2010
  824.912--dc22

                    2010020499

There is a reality outside the world, that is to say, outside space and time, outside man's mental universe, outside any sphere whatsoever that is accessible to human faculties.

Corresponding to this reality, at the centre of the human heart, is the longing for an absolute good, a longing which is always there and is never appeased by any object in this world.

Simone Weil

IN MEMORY OF
JACK MUGGERIDGE
(1909 – 2001)

Table of Contents

MISSIONARIES
OF CHARITY

54 A A.J.C. Bose Road
Calcutta   7700016
INDIA
17 January 1995

Jesus' words spoken from the cross, 'I THIRST,' are written on the wall of every chapel of the Missionaries of Charity throughout the world. When I think of Malcolm Muggeridge, I hear again the words 'I THIRST.'

Jesus thirsted for Malcolm to know Him as truth and as love. He kept calling Malcolm and year by year drew him closer to Himself. Malcolm too thirsted for Jesus, though he was not always aware of it, especially in the beginning. Yet it was God he was looking for, and he was never satisfied with less. What a joy it was for Jesus and for Malcolm when they were united in the Sacraments of the Church. Now, I trust, Malcolm's thirst for Jesus and Jesus' thirst for Malcolm are fully satisfied in heaven.

But Malcolm helped to quench the thirst of Jesus for love in another way. Malcolm is the one who made our works of love for the poorest of the poor known first. Through him, many have come to know the joy of loving and serving Jesus in the poor, and many have even dedicated their lives to Jesus as Sisters and Brothers because of the grace that was channelled to them through his book. And so I thank Jesus, and I thank Malcolm, and I pray that this new book will bring the love of Jesus to many more souls.

God bless you

M Teresa

MC

Introduction

+>=<+

'How to understand? What did it mean? What was the significance?' These were the questions Malcolm Muggeridge put to himself as he pondered the longhaired priests and the muted congregation of a crowded church service in Rostov-on-Don in 1933. Defying the authorities, he was travelling, without a guide or any official sanction, through the North Caucasus and the Ukraine - he was the first western journalist to do so - and witnessing the scenes of horror and desolation that resulted from Stalin's terror-famine: 'one of the most monstrous crimes in history, so terrible that people in the future will scarcely be able to believe it ever happened.'

The image of the church, the observer within and the nightmare without, the clamp-down of a compliant media by the government in Moscow, all combine to form a picture, that to me, symbolises the career of arguably the most brilliant and certainly the most controversial journalist of the twentieth century! Never content with mere reportage, Muggeridge sought the significance and the meaning of the events of his time and tried to relate them to eternity. Reaching beyond the ideological platitudes and the utopian fantasies of his contemporaries, he dared again and again, to speak the truth – and unvarnished truth as he was to repeatedly find, is a highly combustible substance.

In the 1930's the intelligentsia of the West were virtually unanimous in acclaiming the Soviet Government as the epitome of progress and enlightenment at the very time that Stalin and his followers were instigating a reign of terror, impossible, even now, to fully comprehend. Between 1930 and 1937 it has been estimated, 14.5 million peasants died as a result of starvation and persecution, yet Bernard Shaw, Sidney and Beatrice Webb, Harold Laski, Julian Huxley, Sir John Maynard and Walter Duranty, along with, as Arthur Koestler once put it: 'thousands of painters and writers and doctors and lawyers and debutantes chanting a diluted version of the Stalinist line', accepted the Dictatorship of the Proletariat's rule (over others) as benign and justified.

Muggeridge, on the other hand – who recognised the true nature of Bolshevism and accurately reported the Ukrainian famine-genocide of 1932-1933 in which between 5 and 7 million people were systematically murdered – was castigated as being a reactionary and a liar and was unable to find work in Britain for a number of years! As it turned out, his subsequent career proved to be no less emotive. Apart from being once targeted by the National Front, spat at in the street and publicly challenged to a fight by a vicar, he was at different times, banned by the South African, Russian and Portuguese authorities from entering their countries and by the BBC from appearing on television; repeatedly anathematised in the press, he was the recipient of not only razor blades and excrement through the post but also accused of anti-Semitism whilst receiving a death threat for being a defender of the Jews!

It is interesting to consider the extent that Muggeridge aroused strong and often adverse reactions. Few who knew him personally could have failed to recognise his sincerity, kindness and generosity. Claud Cockburn once said of him, that 'there has never been a man on God's earth who would do more for you when the chips are down', whilst Wolf Mankowitz remembered him as being, not only 'a great quality journalist' but as someone who cared so little about money that he must have given 'away an enormous proportion' of what he had earned!

So what was it that stirred up so much antagonism and outrage? The answer is I feel, that Muggeridge dared to write and to speak, honestly and even prophetically, in a time of intellectual myopia and humbug! He tried to understand, to find the meaning, the significance of our life here on earth. We, in the scientific age, may feel that we have driven out God and taken responsibility for the destiny of Mankind but we have proved reluctant to have the disastrous consequences of our actions pointed out! Muggeridge was adept at pricking the bubble of pomposity and of revealing the latest notions of progress and enlightenment - no matter how fashionably attired or loudly acclaimed as yet another manifestation of 'The Emperor's New Clothes'.

+≻═≺+

Malcolm Muggeridge was born in Sanderstead, Surrey, on the 24th March 1903, the third of the five sons born to HT

Muggeridge, the pioneer Socialist and Labour MP, and his wife Annie. In 1910 the family moved to 17 Birdhurst Gardens, a house in South Croydon, designed by HT and built by a co-operative. In this more prosperous setting the Fabian activities of the family and the exuberance of the Muggeridge boys – Douglas, Stanley, Malcolm, Eric and Jack – were viewed askance by their more sedate and conservatively minded neighbours. Certainly it was an unusual household, one in which such concepts as the overthrow of capitalism and the inevitable triumph of a virtuous and downtrodden proletariat formed the backdrop of family life. The boys' situation was further complicated by the fact that their father had singled out Malcolm (in whom he felt he had discerned a special brilliance that would outshine the others) to fulfil vicariously all that he had himself, through poverty and circumstance, been denied. This favoured role involved Malcolm in a special relationship with his father, as well as a University education, from which the four other brothers were excluded.

Malcolm immersed himself in his father's beliefs and hopes, sharing with him the expectation of a soon to be realised, Kingdom of Heaven on Earth. Talking at public meetings, or on a small erected platform in Croydon's Surrey Street Market, HT, a skilled orator and pamphleteer – fond of asking how it was that everything belonged to His Majesty except the National Debt – was in Malcolm's eyes, one of the elect, destined to victoriously depose the corrupt and wicked overlords. This innocent view survived into adulthood in the shape of a lasting distrust of power and of those who exercise it, augmented perhaps (after the collapse of the Labour Party in 1931, due to the formation of the National Coalition Government, and with it, HT's hopes) by an unconscious desire to ridicule the enemy his father had failed to overcome.

After attending State schools in Croydon, Malcolm went to Cambridge University. In 1924 he took up a teaching post at the Union Christian Collage, at Alwaye in India, and it was there that he made his first serious attempts at writing. Returning to England in 1927, he met and married Kathleen (Kitty) Rosalind Dobbs, the niece of Beatrice Webb, the Fabian reformer and sociologist. Malcolm had shared a room with Kitty's brother Leonard at Cambridge, and the match delighted Kitty's mother and Aunt Beatrice. Kitty's father though, far from pleased, called out during the wedding: 'You can still get away Kit.' Not surprisingly, given the pervading atmosphere of free thinking and their casual approach to the union (they asked the registrar how one got a divorce) the relationship was for many years a stormy one; yet despite stresses and infidelities on both sides, the marriage survived for more than sixty years and eventually became outstandingly happy.

After a brief stay in Birmingham, the couple sailed for Egypt, where Malcolm succeeded Robert Graves in a teaching post at Cairo University. This was the first of many moves, Kitty later estimated, that she had set up home for them no less than twenty times. Their first son, Leonard, was born in 1928 and upon Malcolm obtaining a post as a junior leader writer on the *Manchester Guardian*, they returned to England in 1930. Two years later they left for the Soviet Union!

Muggeridge arrived in Russia in September 1932 as the *Manchester Guardian's* Moscow correspondent. The British diplomat, Reader Bullard, noted in his diary on 24 March 1933: 'I met Muggeridge. Since he took over I have noticed that the *Guardian*'s reports have been much more outspoken and nearer the truth.' The fact was, that despite Malcolm's idealistic upbringing and initial optimism, he had quickly realised that the Bolshevik regime, far from being benign or just, was in fact a brutal and evil dictatorship.

Having heard rumours that were filtering through to Moscow, of the disastrous consequences of the collectivisation of farming in the Ukraine and the North Caucasus, Muggeridge decided to see for himself and after travelling through the famine stricken areas in mid February, sent back to England three articles (via diplomatic bag to escape censorship) entitled, *The Soviet and the Peasantry: an Observer's Notes* (a full account of this tragedy would not appear until 1986, with the publication of Robert Conquest's *The Harvest of Sorrow*). Malcolm's historic essays, published in the *Manchester Guardian* on the 26th, 27th, 28th March, were, as his biographer Richard Ingrams has written: 'the first contemporaneous account of the famine by a Western journalist. It created considerable alarm in Moscow coming, as it did, at a time when Stalin was conducting a strenuous campaign to receive official recognition by the USA. Malcolm was denounced in the English language propaganda paper the *Moscow Daily News* as a liar and a ban was quickly introduced on journalist's travel in the famine areas. It was to stay in place until the following year. Official alarm was heightened when Malcolm's account of the famine was confirmed by another writer. Gareth Jones, son of a Welsh headmaster, was a former political secretary of Lloyd George and a fluent Russian speaker who in 1933 went on a walking tour of Russia. His findings were reported in the Guardian on the 30 March 1933.'

Gareth Jones, who had foreseen the inevitability of a famine the pervious year, arrived in Moscow at the beginning of March, and after having gone to meet Muggeridge, decided to see the devastation for himself. His reports published in a number of newspapers on the 30th and 31st of March fully corroborated what Malcolm had written. The Russian authorities immediately put pressure on other western journalists in Moscow to repudiate these accounts - Reader Bullard's diary mentions in July, how a 'prominent communist' had 'raved against Muggeridge for his anti-Soviet articles' - while Malcolm, after furiously remonstrating with W P Crozier, the *Guardian's* editor, for toning down his reports, found himself out of a job.

Muggeridge left Russia in the spring of 1933, joining Kitty in Switzerland where she had gone to give birth to their second son John in February - a daughter, Valentine, was born in 1934 and a third son, Charles, in 1935. After managing to get a job at the International Labour Office in Geneva, Malcolm set about finishing his acclaimed novel *Winter in Moscow* and writing a series of articles for the Morning Post entitled *Russia Revealed*. Ideologically now an outsider and temporally unable to find work in England, Muggeridge managed to obtain a position on the *Calcutta Statesman*. He sailed for India in September 1934 at the same time as his novel *Picture Palace* was withdrawn due to a libel action by his erstwhile employers at the *Manchester Guardian*. In Calcutta he finished a highly critical biography of Samuel Butler, but by the time it was published in 1936, he was back in England working on the Londoner's Diary section of the *Evening Standard*.

The years leading up to the Second World War were spent in Whatlington in Sussex reviewing books, writing a religiously introspective novel, *In a Valley of this Restless Mind,* and *The Thirties,* which was finished in a barrack room hut near Aldershot after he had joined the army as a private. Recruited into MI6, Muggeridge served in North Africa and later in France during the 'Liberation' of Paris, where in the prevailing atmosphere of recrimination, he did all he could to help the scapegoats; two of whom, P G Wodehouse and his wife Ethel - caught up in the furore over Wodehouse's innocent but misunderstood broadcasts from Berlin - became his lifelong friends.

Returning to civilian life after the war, Muggeridge found a job on the *Daily Telegraph,* which took him to America as Washington correspondent in 1946, and subsequently back to London as deputy editor in 1948. By 1953 he had become editor of *Punch,* an uncongenial appointment that had the effect of escalating his appearances on radio and television, where he gained a reputation for the unorthodoxy of his opinions and his exceptional gifts as a broadcaster. This notoriety culminated in a particularly ferocious press campaign against him, provoked by an article he had written on the Monarchy. This article (not by any means his best, as he said himself) was published in America in 1957, shortly after he had resigned from *Punch,* and was widely misquoted in England. Banned by the BBC as a result, and seemingly viewed by a large section of the British public, with disfavour, if not odium, Muggeridge took a year's sabbatical, visiting Australia, China, America and the USSR.

By the 1960's Muggeridge was rehabilitated as far as the television authorities were concerned, and he returned to the BBC via Granada Television, receiving immense exposure throughout the next two decades as a brilliant and often caustic interviewer and documentary maker. Unfortunately, television fame swiftly produces a stereotypical image and Muggeridge, whose espousal of Christianity was becoming increasingly public and whose experience of life made him pessimistic of the success of either sexual or political revolution, became caricatured in the media as an ageing Jeremiah, lashing out against the sensuality and youthful folly he could no longer enjoy. It is worth remembering though, the hothouse atmosphere of the period, when the unscrupulous and the untalented managed to dominate the arts by using every means available to shock and cause outrage. By 1976 even Henry Miller (hardly a prude) had been provoked into exclaiming: 'Sexual revolution? Linda Lovelace? Oh I consider it a misfortune for us that we have created these things....Really I am amazed and disgusted.'

One positive result however, of Malcolm's emergence as an international television personality was an increased demand for his books. Although he had written prolifically in the 40s and 50s (with the exception of the war years), his only publications, apart from his journalistic output after *The Thirties* (1940) were *Affairs of the Heart*, a novel (1949), and *About Kingsmill* (1954), a tribute to his friend the writer Hugh Kingsmill, written in collaboration with Hesketh Pearson. In the 60's and 70's coinciding with the reissue of much of his earlier work, he produced some of his most powerful writing in which he related Christ's teaching to the circumstance of modern life from a non-denominational perspective, finding a large response among people of all ages and backgrounds, including many who felt separated from the mainstream of Christian churchgoers.

The T'ang poet Han Shan (circa 800AD) wrote in one of his Cold Mountain poems, of evil and corrupt Buddhist priests driving people away from their religion:

'What a fine shop this is!
And the wine they sell is the best around.
- What's that? You complain your sales are poor?
But then, you will keep the place full of vicious dogs!
No sooner has a fellow come in for a drink
Than they snap at his heels and drive him away.'

(Translation: Burton Watson)

In our own time, in addition to the shortcomings of some clergy, the espousal of Jesus by people who can appear somewhat over-confident of their own salvation and to have much in common with the Pharisee at the front of the temple thanking God he was not like the sinful publican at the back has had the unfortunate effect of not only driving people away from the Gospels but of making the very word 'Christian' represent, to some, an innocuous and sanctimonious view of life. In books such as *Jesus Rediscovered, Jesus the Man who Lives*, and *The Third Testament,* Muggeridge spoke to many who were alienated in this way and who recognised that here was someone with genuine insight who spoke to them directly and honestly.

In 1967, Malcolm visited the Holy Land where he wrote and narrated a film for the BBC on the life of Christ. About this time he began to question his non-denominational stance after meeting two Catholics who were each exemplifying in their own way, what Jack Kerouac has called the 'seed soul' of Christianity: 'Care and Reverence' - Fr Paul Bidone, an Italian priest working with handicapped children and the aged, and Agnes Bojaxhiu, known as Mother Teresa.

Muggeridge travelled to India in 1968, to make a documentary about Mother Teresa and the order of nuns that she had founded. The film, *Something Beautiful for God* and its accompanying book of the same name are both moving documents that have made their work amongst the poorest of the poor, amongst victims of leprosy, and abandoned children, known all over the world.

The subject matter, one would have thought, was of a sort least likely to arouse controversy. Eventually however, the respect and renown that Mother Teresa was accorded worldwide, proved too much of a temptation to a few individuals who - perhaps thinking to emulate Herostatus, the man in Ancient Greece who burnt down the Temple of Artemis (one of the seven wonders of the world) in order to immortalise his name - began to attack her. Muggeridge, naturally, was hit by some of the fall-out from these attacks and, beneath contempt as such behaviour obviously is, one example might be worth mentioning: In the course of filming *Something Beautiful for God*, some footage shot in Nirmal Hriday, the Home for the Dying, which the crew were convinced would prove unusable because of the poor visibility - footage shot in similar conditions in Cairo shortly afterwards, with the same film-stock, and by the same cameraman, proved completely unusable – turned out, when processed, to be bathed in a particularly beautiful light.

Malcolm saw it in this way: 'I myself am absolutely convinced that the technically unaccountable light is, in fact, the Kindly Light Newman refers to in his well-known exquisite hymn. – Mother Teresa's Home for the Dying is overflowing with love, as one senses immediately on entering it. This love is luminous, like the haloes artists have seen and made visible round the heads of the saints. I find it not at all surprising that the luminosity should register on a photographic film. The supernatural is only an infinite projection of the natural, as the furthest horizon is an image of eternity, Jesus put mud on a blind man's eyes and made him see. It was a beautiful gesture, showing that he could bring out even in mud its innate power to heal and enrich. All the wonder and glory of mud – year by year giving creatures their food, and our eyes the delight of flowers and trees and blossoms – was crystallised to restore sight to unseeing eyes.'

To quibble with this enchanting passage and to try to ridicule Muggeridge for it, as some people have done, seems to me to be wilfully obtuse. I am reminded of how Charles Lamb, who when a son of Robert Burns was expected at a gathering, remarked that he wished it was the father instead of the son and was confronted by four of the company jumping up to say that that was impossible because he was dead. Malcolm's response was essentially an artistic and imaginative one. To question the light in the Home of the Dying factually, is to miss the point. Muggeridge (who had once interviewed a rather back-sliding bishop on location, whose every second word was punctuated by a cock crowing) accepted that

God's hand could stoop to ripple even the muddy waters of television, and felt that the light Mother Teresa was shining was so bright that it could impinge itself, even on film, if not make the very stones cry out. He of course realised, that as Simone Weil once wrote: 'A gift of alms out of pure charity is as great a marvel as walking on water' and would have happily concurred with the producer of the film, Peter Chafer's statement, that if there was a genuine miracle in Calcutta, it was walking around in sandals and was in fact the subject of the documentary.

From a personal point of view I can say this – that during the time that it was my good fortune to know Malcolm and Kitty Muggeridge, I found them to be anything but fanciful, remarkably down to earth and completely unpretentious. To give one example: When I turned up unexpectedly at their cottage in Sussex one afternoon in 1981 – having corresponded briefly with Malcolm – I was invited in and treated with wonderful courtesy. They were so relaxed in fact, that I did not realise that they were in fact in the middle of an important photo shoot for a forthcoming *Observer* newspaper front-page spread, and that the celebrated photographer Jane Bown was outside investigating possible locations.

Only when, a half hour later, someone came in the front door and Kitty went out to speak to her, did I realise that something was going on. Malcolm, however, carried on chatting completely naturally, giving no indication that he had more important things on hand. It was not until I stood up and said that I would not take up any more of their time, that Malcolm too, got up and taking me out into the hall, introduced me to Ms Bown, saying that I was an old friend of theirs, and how glad they were that I had dropped in to see them. It was beautifully done, and kindly done. A day or so later, I received a letter from them both, asking me to come and see them again with my wife and family. It was crystal clear on that first afternoon and on our subsequent meetings, that not a hint of that self-importance, that surreptitiously seems to envelop almost everyone in the public eye, had touched them.

In 1982 Malcolm and Kitty were received into the Catholic Church, citing Mother Teresa as a major influence in their decision. In his last book *Conversion* (1988) Malcolm wrote that he had found her insistence on treating all human beings as if they were Jesus, irresistible, adding that there had been no book that he had ever read, or transcendental experience that had ever befallen him, that had brought him nearer to Christ or made him more aware of what the incarnation signified, than listening to Mother Teresa and observing her, had done. Malcolm died on the 14th November 1990, and is buried in Whatlington churchyard in East Sussex. Kitty, who died in 1994, is buried with him.

⊹⇒⋯⇐⊹

'It is impossible to scan any periodical,' Charles Baudelaire wrote in the 1860s, 'of whatever day, month or year, without finding in every line of it evidence of the most appalling human perversity, together with the most surprising boasts of probity, goodness and charity and the most shameless assertions concerning progress and civilisation.' In the nineteenth century, as W G De Burgh pointed out, when society seemed to be 'on the upward grade, the humanistic creed could offer a certain plausibility; but today in the light of the widespread disintegration of the bonds of human fellowship and social order, it is surely a paradox that it should retain its power to inspire thinking men.'

'The basis of liberal-humanism,' Muggeridge once wrote is that 'there is no creature in the universe greater than man, and the future of the human race rests only with human beings themselves, which leads infallibly to some sort of suicidal situation. - Once you eliminate the notion of a God, a creator, once you eliminate the notion that the creator has a purpose for us, and that life consists essentially in fulfilling that purpose, then you are bound - to induce the megalomania of which we've seen so many manifestations in our time.'

Malcolm's conversion to Christianity was erroneously seen by many people, as a sea change. He himself put it this way: 'It is generally assumed, by those who know me only through the media, especially television, that for the greater part of my life my attitudes were wholly hedonistic and my ways wholly worldly, until, in my late sixties, I suddenly discovered God and became preoccupied with other-worldly considerations - The fact is - I have never cared much for this present world, and have found its pleasures and prizes, such as they are, little to my taste.'

Muggeridge's earlier, supposedly secular writings, reprinted here, from his denunciation of Stalin's organised famine in the Ukraine, to his assessments of D H Lawrence, Havelock Ellis and other luminaries, all have a distinctly religious flavour. The journals and letters that I uncovered amongst his private papers are manifestly those of a spiritual disposition. The totality of his work displays an acute disquiet at the growing arrogance and apostasy of western men and women and of the disastrous effects of their attempts to establish a Kingdom of Heaven on Earth!

The road Malcolm travelled was a long and sometimes torturous one - stretching from his encounter in Russia with the darkest side of human nature in all its cruelty and horror, to the bright legacy of Mother Teresa and Jesus' Kingdom not of this world. But, as the essays that follow reveal, Mother Teresa was right: 'It was God he was looking for and he was never satisfied with less.' Those of us who would follow in his footsteps can take comfort, as Malcolm often did, in Pascal's words: 'I look for God, therefore I have found him.' Looking back later, in the 1950's, to the land where his journey had taken such a decisive turn, Malcolm's overall feeling was one of gratitude:

'When I think of Russia now I remember, not the grey, cruel set faces of its present masters, but rather how kindly and humorous the people subjected to them managed to remain despite the appalling physical and mental suffering they had to endure. I remember a little painted church standing in the moonlight like an exquisite jewel, someone having managed in inconceivably difficult circumstances to keep its bright colours fresh and triumphant. - Above all, I remember going to an Easter service in Kiev - the crowded cathedral, the overwhelmingly beautiful music, the intense sense which, as they worshipped, the congregation conveyed of eternity sweeping in like great breakers on the crumbling shores of Time.'

1

THE COLLECTIVISATION OF THE UKRAINE

L iving in Moscow and listening always to statements of doctrine and policy, you forget that Moscow is the centre of a country stretching over a sixth of the world's surface and that the lives of a hundred and sixty million people, mostly peasants, are profoundly affected by discussions and resolutions that seem, when you hear or read of them in the press, as abstract as the proceedings of a provincial debating society. 'We must collectivise agriculture', or 'We must root out kulaks' (the rich peasants). How simple it sounds! How logical! But what is going on in the remote villages, in the small households of the peasants? What does this collectivisation of agriculture mean in practice in the lives of the peasantry? What results have the new 'drive' produced? What truth, if any, is there in the gloomy reports that have been reaching Moscow? That is what I wanted to find out. I set out to discover it in the North Caucasus and the Ukraine.

If you fall asleep in Moscow and then wake up and, looking out of a railway carriage window, find yourself in the Ukraine you suddenly feel gay and light-hearted. There are great

17

sweeps of country, and you realise that Moscow is sombre and shut-in. Now you breathe again; now you see a horizon. Only, the way to go over the glistening snow would be not in an overheated railway compartment, with a gramophone playing stale jazz music, but in a sledge drawn by swift horses with silver bells round their necks and with the cold wind against your face.

A little market town in the Kuban district of the North Caucasus suggested a military occupation; worse, active war. There were soldiers everywhere, – Mongols with leaden faces and slit eyes; others obviously peasants, rough but not brutal; occasional officers, dapper, often Jews; all differing noticeably from the civilian population in one respect – they were all well fed and the civilian population were obviously starving. I mean starving in its absolute sense; not undernourished as for instance most Oriental peasants are undernourished or some unemployed workers in Europe, but having had for weeks next to nothing to eat. Later I found out there had been no bread at all in the place for three months, and such food as there was I saw for myself in the market. The only edible thing there of the lowest European standards was chicken – about five chickens, fifteen roubles each. No one was buying. Where could a peasant get fifteen roubles? For the most part, chickens – the few that remain – are sold at the railway stations to passengers on their way to the mountains in the South for a holiday or for a rest cure in a sanatorium.

The rest of the food offered for sale was revolting and would be thought unfit in the ordinary way to be offered even to animals. There was sausage at fifteen roubles the kilo; there was black cooked meat which worked out I calculated at a rouble for three bites; there were miserable fragments of cheese and some cooked potatoes, half rotten. A crowd wandered backwards and forwards eyeing these things wistfully, too poor to buy. The few who bought gobbled their purchases ravenously then and there.

'How are things with you?' I asked one man. He looked round anxiously to see that no soldiers were about. 'We have nothing, absolutely nothing. They have taken everything away', he said, and hurried on. This was what I heard again and again and again. 'We have nothing. They have taken everything away'. It was quite true. They had nothing. It was also true that everything had been taken away. The famine is an organised one. Some of the food that has been taken away from them – and the peasants know this quite well – is still being exported to foreign countries.

It is impossible adequately to describe the melancholy atmosphere of this little market town; how derelict it was; the sense of hopelessness pervading the place, and this was not just because the population was, as it were, torn up by the roots. The class war has been waged vigorously in the North Caucasus, and the proletariat, represented by the G.P.U. (State Political Police) and the military, has utterly routed its enemies amongst the peasantry who tried to hide a little of their produce to feed themselves through the winter. Despite hostile elements, however, the North Caucasus distinguished itself by being 90 per cent collectivised, and then this year by fulfilling its grain delivery plan. As a result, this double effort has turned it into something like a wilderness – fields choked with weeds, cattle dead, people starving and dispirited, no horses for ploughing or transport, not even adequate supplies of seed for the spring sowing. The worst of the class war is that it never stops. First individual kulaks shot and exiled; then groups of peasants; then whole villages. I walked from street to street watching the faces of people, looking at empty shops. Even here a Torgsin shop; good food offered for gold; useful for locating any private hoards that organised extortion had failed to detect.

The little villages round about were even more depressing than the market town. Often they seemed quite deserted. Only smoke coming from some of the chimneys told they were populated. In one of the larger villages I counted only five people in the street, and there was a soldier riding up and down on - a rare sight now in the North Caucasus - a fine horse. It is literally true that whole villages have been exiled. In some cases demobilised soldiers have been moved in to the places of the exiles; in some cases the houses are just left empty. I saw myself a group of some twenty peasants being marched off under escort. This is so common a sight it no longer even arouses curiosity. Everywhere I heard that the winter sowing had been miserably done, and that in any case the land was too weed-ridden to yield even a moderate crop. Though it was winter, in some places weeds still stood - taller than wheat and growing thickly. There were no cattle to be seen, and I was assured that in that part of the North Caucasus at least, there were none at all. They had been killed and eaten or died of starvation.

Occasionally along the road I met with little groups of peasants with rifles slung over their shoulders; men in fur caps, rough looking; a kind of armed militia that has also been mobilised on the kulak front. I wanted to find out about future prospects; whether the change from forced grain collections to a more moderately assessed tax-in-kind was going to make things better; what chances there were even now of retrieving the blunders of the last two years. It is difficult, however, to get people who are starving and who know that whatever happens, they must go on starving for at least three more months, and probably five, to talk about or take any great interest in the future. To them the question of bread, of how to get the food to keep just alive today and tomorrow, transcends all others. Starving people are not in a general way loquacious, particularly when to talk may be to qualify as a kulak and so for exile or worse. I was shown a piece of bread from Stavropol. It was made, I was told, of weeds and straw and a little millet. It seemed inconceivable that anyone could eat such bread; actually in the circumstances a rare delicacy.

The peasants in this region had to provide exports to pay for the Five-Year Plan; they had to be – to use an expression of Stalin's in a lecture on the peasant question – 'reserves of the proletariat'; and the 'reserves' had to be mobilised, made accessible – that is collectivised. It was not difficult for the Soviet Government to make collectivisation, in the quantitative sense, an enormous success – so enormous that even the Communist Party grew a little anxious and Stalin issued a public warning against 'business from success'. In the event about 60 per cent of the peasantry and 80 per cent of the land were brought into collective farms; Communists with impeccable ideology were installed as directors of them; agronomes were to provide expert advice, tractors to replace horses, elevators to replace barns, and the practice of America combined with the theory of Marxism was to transform agriculture into a kind of gigantic factory staffed by an ardently class-conscious proletariat.

As things turned out the Communist directors were sometimes incompetent or corrupt; the agronomes, despite their scientific training, were in many cases a failure in dealing with the actual problems connected with producing food; horses died off for lack of fodder much faster than tractors were manufactured, and the tractors were mishandled and broken; the attitude of the peasants varied from actual sabotage or passive resistance to mere apathy, and was generally, to say the least, unhelpful; altogether in the qualitative sense, collectivisation was a failure. The immediate result was, of course, a falling off in the yield of agriculture as a whole. Last year this falling off became acute. None the less the Government quota had to be collected. To feed the cities and to provide even very much reduced food exports it was necessary for the Government's agents to go over the country and take everything, or nearly everything, that was edible. At the same time, because the policy could not be wrong and therefore individuals and classes had to be at fault, there took place a new outburst of repression, directed this time not only against the kulaks but against every kind of peasant suspected of opposing the Government's policy; against a good number of directors and the unfortunate agronomes. Shebboldaev, party secretary for the North Caucasus, said in a speech delivered at Rostov on November 12:

'But, you may urge, is it not true that we have deported kulaks and counter-revolutionary elements before? We did deport them, and in sufficiently large numbers. But at the present moment, when what remains of the kulaks are trying to organise sabotage, every slacker must be deported. That is true justice. You may say that before, we exiled individual kulaks, and that now it concerns whole stanitzas (villages) and whole collective farms. If these are enemies they must be treated as kulaks. . . The general line of our party is to fight dishonesty by means of the extreme penalty, because this is the only defence we have against the destruction of our so-cialist economy'.

It is this 'true justice' that has helped greatly to reduce the North Caucasus to its present condition.

My train reached Rostov-on-Don – a fairly large town, capital of the North Caucasus – in the early morning before it was even light. I had been travelling 'hard' and trying to find out from some of the peasants in a crowded compartment where they were going and why. Many appeared to have no particular object in view; just a vague hope that things might be better somewhere else. In Russia, as in most other parts of the world, there is much aimless movement just now from one place to another. One peasant however had a specific object; he wanted to join the army because, he said, one was fed in the army. On the platform a group of peasants were standing in military formation; five soldiers armed with rifles guarded them. They were men and women, each carrying a bundle. Somehow, lining them up in military formation made the thing grotesque – wretched looking peasants, half-starved, tattered clothes, frightened faces, standing to attention. These may be kulaks, I thought, but they have made a mighty poor thing of exploiting their fellows. I hung about looking on curiously, wanting to ask where they were to be sent – to the North to cut timber, somewhere else to dig canals – until one of the guards told me sharply to take myself off.

In Rostov I had a letter of introduction, which I presented, and found myself in a large car with a guide. 'There we're building new Government offices, eight stories high; there a new theatre and opera house to seat 3,000, with living quarters behind for the actors; a new factory that three years ago didn't exist, blocks of flats for the workers, the latest machinery and sanitation'. I began to forget the group of peasants being lined up in military formation on a cold railway platform in the very early morning. Showmanship – most characteristic product of the age – worked its magic. 'Have you got bread here in Rostov?' I asked weakly. 'Bread? Of course we've got bread; as much as we can eat'. It was not true but they had a certain amount of bread. One might go all over Russia like this, I thought – on a wave of showmanship. It explained something that has so often puzzled me.

How is it that so many obvious and fundamental facts about Russia are not noticed even by serious and intelligent visitors? Take, for instance, the most obvious and fundamental fact of all. There is not 5 per cent of the population whose standard of life is equal to or nearly equal to, that of the unemployed in England who are on the lowest scales of relief. I make this statement advisedly, having checked it on the basis of the family budgets in Mr. Fenner Brockway's recent book *Hungry England,* which certainly did not err on the side of being too optimistic.

In the evening I joined a crowd in a street. It was drifting up and down while a policeman was blowing his whistle; dispersing just where he was and re-forming again behind him. Some of the people in the crowd were holding fragments of food, inconsiderable fragments that in the ordinary way a housewife would throw away or give to the cat. Others were examining these fragments of food. Every now and then an exchange took place. Often, as in the little market town, what was bought was at once consumed. I turned into a nearby church. It was crowded. A service was proceeding; priests in vestments and with long hair were chanting prayers, little candle flames lighting the darkness, incense rising. How to understand? How to form an opinion? What did it mean? What was the significance? The voices of the priests were dim, like echoes, and the congregation curiously quiet, curiously still.

I dined with a number of Communists. They were so friendly and sincere. 'About this peasant business?' I asked. They smiled, having an answer ready. 'As the factories were in 1920 so now the farms. We've built up heavy industry; the next task is agriculture. Fifteen collective farm workers have gone to Moscow to a conference. Comrade Stalin will address them. This year we will plant so many hectares, which will produce so many pounds of grain. Then next year...'

'Are you quite sure', I wanted to ask, 'that the parallel is correct – factories and land? Isn't agriculture somehow more sensitive, lending itself less to statistical treatment? Will people torn up by the roots make things grow, even if you drive them into the fields at the end of a rifle?' It is, however, as impossible to argue against a General Idea as against an algebraic formula.

The Ukraine is more a separate country than the North Caucasus. It has a language of its own and an art of its own; southern rather than eastern, with white, good houses and easy-going people. Even now you can see it has been used to abundance. There is nothing pinchbeck about the place; only as in the North Caucasus, the population is starving. 'Hunger' was the word I heard most. Peasants begged a lift on the train from one station to another, sometimes their bodies swollen up - a disagreeable sight - from lack of food. There were fewer signs of military terrorism than in the North Caucasus, though I saw another party of, presumably, kulaks being marched away under an armed guard at Dnipropetrovsk; the little towns and villages seemed just numb and the people in too desperate a condition to even actively resent what had happened.

Otherwise it was the same story - cattle and horses dead; fields neglected, meagre harvests despite moderately good climatic conditions; all the grain that was produced taken by the Government; no bread at all, no bread anywhere, nothing much else either; despair and bewilderment. The Ukraine was before the Revolution one of the world's largest wheat producing areas, and even Communists admit that its population, including the poor peasants, enjoyed a tolerably comfortable standard of life; now it would be necessary to go to Arabia to find cultivators in more wretched circumstances. Here too, there are new factories, a huge new power station at Dnieprostroi, a huge new square at Kharkov with huge Government buildings - and food being exported from Odessa.

In a village about 25 kilometres from Kyiv (old capital of the Ukraine – enchanting town – now Kharkov is the capital) I visited a collective farm worker or *kolhoznik*. His wife was in the outer room of their cottage sifting millet. There were also three chickens in the outer room, and on the wall two icons, a bouquet made of coloured paper and a wedding group, very gay.

'How are things?' I asked.

'Bad', she answered.

'Why?'

'Only potatoes and millet to eat since August'.

'No bread or meat?'

'None'.

'Were things better before you joined the collective farm?'

'Much better'.

'Why did you join, then?'

'Oh, I don't know'.

She opened a door leading to an inner room to call her husband. He was lying on the stove, but got up when she called and came in to us carrying one child and with another following him. Both children were obviously undernourished. I told the man that I was interested in collective farms, and he was ready to talk. 'I was a poor peasant', he said, 'with a hectare and a half of land. I thought that things would be better for me on the collective farm'.

'Well, were they?'

He laughed, 'Not at all; much worse'.

'Worse than before the Revolution?'

He laughed again. 'Much, much worse. Before the Revolution we had a cow and something to feed it with; plenty of bread, meat sometimes. Now nothing but potatoes and millet'.

'What's happened, then? Why is there no bread in the Ukraine?'

'Bad organisation. They send people from Moscow who know nothing; ordered us here to grow vegetables instead of wheat. We didn't know how to grow vegetables and they couldn't show us. Then we were told that we must put our cows all together and there'd be plenty of milk for our children, but the expert who advised this forgot to provide a cow shed, so we had to put our cows in the sheds of the rich peasants, who, of course, let them starve'.

'I thought you'd got rid of all the rich peasants?'

'We did but their agents remain'.

'What about the winter sowing?'

'Very bad'.

'Why?'

'Again bad organisation. People lost heart and stopped working. Weeds everywhere, and, with the cattle dead, no manure; no horses to transport fertiliser, even if it was available'. He hushed his voice, 'There are enemies even on the Council of the collective farm. Now, they wouldn't elect me to the Council'.

'Some grain must have been produced. What happened to it?'

'All taken by the Government'.

'It'll be better in that respect this year. You'll only have to pay tax-in-kind - so much per hectare - and not deliver a quota for the whole district. When you've paid the tax-in-kind you'll have about two-thirds of the crop left to yourselves'.

'If we get as big a crop as they estimate. But we shan't – not with the land in such a bad condition and with no horses. They'll take everything again'.

He showed me his time-book. His pay was seventy-five ko-peks a day. At open market prices seventy-five kopeks would buy half a slice of bread. He said that for the most part he spent the money on fuel. Sometimes he bought a little tobac-co. Nothing else. No clothes, of course, or boots, or anything like that.

'What about the future?' I asked. He put on a characteristic peasant look; half resignation and half cunning.

'We shall see'.

<hr />

When I got back to Moscow I found that Stalin had deliv-ered himself of this opinion to a conference of collective farm shock-brigade workers:

'By developing collective farming we succeeded in draw-ing this entire mass of poor peasants into collective farms, in giving them security and raising them to the level of middle peasants . . . what does this mean? It means that no less than 30,000,000 of the peasant population have been saved from poverty and from kulak slavery, and converted, thanks to col-lective farms, into people assured of a livelihood. This is a great achievement, comrades. This is an achievement such as the world has never known and such as not a single State in the world has ever before secured'.

All the available evidence goes to show that conditions in the Upper, Middle and Lower Volga districts are as bad as in the North Caucasus and the Ukraine; in Western Siberia they are little, if at all, better. No one knows what supplies of grain the Government has at its disposal, but as I have already pointed out, the food situation cannot improve before the summer and is likely to deteriorate. The spring sowing will be a critical time; all the resources of the Government and the Communist Party are to be used to make it a success. Already intensive propaganda is being carried on, and 'political departments', manned chiefly by the military and the G.P.U., have been brought into existence in all parts of the country. These will be responsible for executing the Government's policy and, of course, vigorously carrying on the class war.

Even so, will it suffice? Will it suffice, even assuming the best possible conditions – good weather, the peasants propagandised, cajoled and coerced into working well, sufficient tractors repaired and properly handled to make good to some extent the lost horses, everyone, including town populations, mobilised for clearing weeds, enough seed made available and so on? As one says complacently of so much else in Russia, it will be an interesting experiment – interesting, that is, for the onlooker; for the actual participators often more disagreeable than interesting. In any case, it is certainly true that, unless the decay of agriculture that began when the collectivisation policy was first started and that has gone on at an increasing rate ever since, is stopped; unless, that is to say, the Government is able to produce a better crop this year than last, there will be famine not merely in certain districts but throughout the country.

It was strange in a way to return to Moscow, where the General Idea reigns supreme and where you have no alternative but to take it for granted. There can seldom have been in the history of the world a more curious tyranny than the Soviet regime – not just personal, based on an individual's or a group of individuals' appetite for absolute power; not an autocracy like, for instance, the British Raj in India, based on expediency, on there being no other way of dealing with a particularly confused set of social circumstances; but a tyranny that developed inevitably out of a General Idea and that can, by its very nature, only become more and more absolute. The Dictatorship of the Proletariat has come to mean the Dictatorship of the Communist Party; and the Dictatorship of the Communist Party has come to mean the Dictatorship of the Polit-Bureau; and the Dictatorship of the Polit-Bureau has come to mean the Dictatorship of Stalin; the Dictatorship of Stalin has come to mean the Dictatorship of the General Idea with which he is obsessed. If the General Idea is fulfilled it can only be by bringing into existence a slave State.

The tendency in Russia is towards a slave State. First the old aristocracy and bourgeoisie were enslaved. Who cared about that? They had their day, abused their privileges, and it was fitting that they should cut timber and dig canals for the proletariat they had tyrannised. But when the old aristocracy and bourgeoisie had been enslaved the General Idea was as far from fulfilment as ever. It can only be fulfilled when it dominates the lives of the whole population. And since the vast majority of men resist such a domination they must be forced to submit. Fear forces them – fear of losing their bread rations; fear of being driven from where they live; fear of being informed against to the police. The present battle is between the General Idea and the peasants.

I arrived back in Moscow to find the newspapers full of reports of speeches by various members of the Government about the agricultural situation that had been delivered to a Conference of the Collective Farm Shock-Brigade Workers. It is impossible, through the censorship, to comment on these speeches, which bear no relation at all to the realities of the situation. To say that there is famine in some of the most fertile parts of Russia is to say much less than the truth; there is not only famine but - in the case of the North Caucasus at least - a state of war, a military occupation. In both the Ukraine and the North Caucasus the grain collection has been carried out with such thoroughness and brutality that the peasants are now quite without bread. Thousands of them have been exiled; in certain cases whole villages have been sent to the North for forced labour; even now it is a common sight to see parties of wretched men and women, labelled kulaks, being marched away under an armed guard.

The fields are neglected and full of weeds; no cattle are to be seen anywhere, and few horses; only the military and the GPU are well fed, the rest of the population obviously starving, obviously terrorised. There is no hope - at least until the summer - of conditions improving. In fact they must get worse. The winter sowing has been neglected. Only a small area has been sown at all, and that badly. The general condition of the land and the lack of transport make it unlikely, whatever efforts the government may make, that the spring sowing will be much better.

At the conference there were violent outbursts against the kulaks. Where failure existed they were responsible; they had falsified the accounts, hidden grain, broken machines, organised sabotage and passive resistance against the Government. But for them the peasants would have faithfully yielded up all they had produced and then have waited patiently through the winter, with little or nothing to eat, to do the same things again this year. Our new slogan, Stalin said, must be to make every collective farm worker well-to-do. It is an admirable slogan; to judge, however, by the facts of the case, the Government's slogan would seem to have been hitherto to take from every collective farm worker everything he had – even the minimum amount of food required for his own and his family's consumption.

In any case, the Government's policy is based not on persuasion or concession but on force. 'Political departments', manned chiefly by GPU. and military, have been set up all over the country, and these will be responsible for raising and collecting a harvest. They will drive the peasants into the fields; they will make them work; they will collect most of what they produce. If necessary they will mobilise town populations for work on the land, as by a decree published in an Archangel newspaper, the whole population in that district was mobilised to cut timber because the export quota was unfulfilled. The spring sowing will be carried out, if at all, as a result of coercion. The Government realises at last how serious the situation is, and, to deal with it, employs its familiar tactics - speeches, slogans, enthusiastic conferences in Moscow; in the villages, ruthless, organised force.

2

THE SOUL OF BOLSHEVISM

M arxism is the most urban religion that has ever existed. It was born in underground printing presses, in squalid London lodgings, in dingy cafés and third-rate hotels; its prophets were wanderers from one European capital to another whose dreams, like themselves, were rootless, took no account of earth or of things growing or of allegiances; not having any contact with civilisation, hating civilisation, they saw the future as do some capitalists – their prototypes – in terms of machines and papers and columns of grey, regimented men and women who shout obedient slogans and build mechanically a hideous paradise.

What the Bolsheviks have done in the towns of Russia is nothing; a kind of inverted American boom; a kind of morbid equivalent of the general post-war economic extravagance; a thing that might pass and be quickly forgotten. The particular horror of their rule is what they have done in the villages. This, I am convinced, is one of the most monstrous crimes in history, so terrible that people in the future will scarcely be able to believe it ever happened.

If you go now to the Ukraine or the North Caucasus, exceedingly beautiful countries and formerly amongst the most fertile in the world, you will find them like a desert; fields choked with weeds and neglected; no livestock or horses; villages seeming to be deserted, sometimes actually deserted; peasants famished, often their bodies swollen, unutterably wretched. You will discover, if you question them, that they have had no bread at all for three months past; only potatoes and some millet, and that now they are counting their potatoes one by one because they know nothing else will be available to eat until the summer, if then. They will tell you that many have already died of famine, and that many are dying every day; that thousands have been shot by the government and hundreds of thousands exiled; that it is a crime, punishable by the death sentence without trial, for them to have grain in their houses.

They will only tell you these things, however, if no soldier or stranger is within sight. At the sight of a uniform or of someone properly fed, whom they assume, because of that fact, to be a Communist or a Government official, they change their tone and assure you that they have everything in the way of food and clothing that the heart of man can desire, and that they love the dictatorship of the proletariat, and recognise thankfully the blessings it has brought to them. Strange as it may seem, a certain number of these poor wretches are from time to time made to speak in this strain to parties of tourists. I found that the name of Bernard Shaw was known to them. They spoke of him privately in the same tone, and spitting as venomously, as when they spoke of Stalin.

I saw these conditions for myself in the North Caucasus and the Ukraine, and heard from many sources, some Russian, some foreign, and some even Communist, that similar conditions prevailed in all the agricultural districts of Russia. This is unquestionably the case. It is impossible to describe the horror of it. I saw in India villages devastated by cholera. It was terrible. They were dead villages. Yet plagues pass, and I knew that the villages would fill again with living people. I saw in Belgium villages devastated by war. They, too, were dead villages. Yet even the war had ended, and I knew that the villages would fill again with living people. Villages devastated by the Bolsheviks were terrible beyond words because there seemed no end. It was as though a blight had settled on the country. It was a though nothing would ever grow there again. It was as though the peasants, their lives torn up by the roots, were ghosts haunting a place where they had once lived and been happy.

Why should it ever stop? I asked myself – soldiers, impersonal, some of them Mongols with leaden faces and slit eyes; members of the GPU, dapper, well-fed, often Jews, carrying out the orders of the dictatorship of the proletariat, destroying more surely than barbarians (who come with sword and fire, things relatively clean) the life, the soul of a country. Why should it ever stop until there is no class-enemy left to destroy – that is, no-one left; and no grain left to collect because none planted? Thinking it over afterwards, I came to the conclusion that the thing could only be explained on the supposition that the dictatorship of the proletariat hated Russia and was determined to destroy Russia even though thereby it also destroyed itself.

From the beginning, the Bolsheviks have regarded the peasants as so much raw material for carrying out their plans. They gave them the land in order to get power, and, having got power, took the land away from them. After the famine of 1921; after the Kronstadt revolt, when those whom Trotsky had called 'the pride and the glory of the Revolution' demanded, amongst other things, free elections and a secret ballot; liberty of speech and of the Press for workers and peasants; the right to organise Trade Unions; equal rations for all who worked; and when they were, in consequence, shot down in hundreds by Trotsky's orders, and then handed over to the GPU, that had run away when the revolt started, for an orgy of sadistic revenge – after all this, the peasants were given the right to trade freely with their produce. As soon, however, as they began to grow prosperous again, the promises that had been made to them were broken. Those peasants who, because they were more industrious or more unscrupulous or more intelligent than their fellows, had prospered, were treated as dangerous criminals; the New Economic Policy, like the Torgsin shops, was a means of locating thrift and wealth in order to destroy the one and steal the other.

Collectivisation and de-kulakisation followed. The peasants were driven, mostly at the end of a rifle, into collective farms, which, being incompetently and often corruptly directed by picked Communists, have failed to produce enough food to feed the town populations, let alone provide exports to pay for Socialist construction. Last autumn and winter the Government's agents went over the country like a swarm of locusts taking everything edible, and leaving behind them a desert. The dictatorship of the proletariat has entrusted the task of making this desert fruitful again to its 'flaming sword,' the GPU which, under the name of 'political departments' established in every machine-tractor-station and State farm – that is, everywhere – will attempt to produce crops by the same methods as those by which timber has been produced for export.

To all intents and purposes the whole peasantry has been arrested and sentenced to forced labour. The proletariat's 'flaming sword' is at its best in dealing with helpless, unorganised, starved people; even so, a hundred million peasants may well prove unmanageable. If not, if, under the patronage of 'political departments,' the fields bear abundantly, then a new and most hideous kind of slavery will have to be reckoned with, a slavery different from, and more awful than, any hitherto known in the world.

<hr />

In the centre of Moscow and opposite the Foreign Office, which is in every sense of the word a sort of annex to it, stands the headquarters of the GPU – a solid building; the best designed and most substantially built in Russia since the Revolution; equipped with offices, a prison, a slaughter-house, an excellently stocked restaurant and multiple store reserved exclusively for its personnel. Altogether a comfortable, attractive place, always busy, always with people passing in and out, mostly men in uniform, very smart, very important looking, very contemptuous in their manner towards what Trotsky speaks of so often and so affectionately in his 'History of the Russian Revolution' as the 'broad' or 'toiling' masses. It need scarcely be said that this building is not one which tourists are shown over when they visit Moscow.

The GPU embodies all the fear, all the distrust, all the passion to be revenged on society, all the hatred of civilisation and of human happiness that lives in the soul of Bolshevism. It is the soul of Bolshevism; and as time goes on, as the trivial hypocrisies in which Bolshevism has dressed itself - in order to deceive and flatter and use for its purposes the frustrated intellectuals of civilised Europe and uncivilised America - tend to get thrown aside, it emerges as the ultimate authority in Russia, the very dictatorship of the proletariat.

No one who has not seen it for himself can understand the terror that this organisation inspires, not merely in avowed enemies of the Soviet régime - ex-bourgeoisie, priests, people who were for any reason privileged under the old social order - but in the whole population. It is not so much that they dread what the GPU may do to them, though it can do anything without anyone, even their nearest relatives, knowing; they dread the thing itself, because of its nature, because it is utterly evil, because it is morbid, because it belongs to those fearful distortions and perversions that exist in all human beings, but that, in a civilised society, emerge only occasionally in some criminal or madman.

I often used to think, when I was in Russia, that the general attitude towards the GPU must be like the general attitude in the Middle Ages towards the Powers of Darkness - quite irrational; quite unrelated to knowledge or experience of its manner of working; yet somehow understandable, somehow in keeping with the facts of the case. There is, mixed up with it all, a kind of mysticism. I turned up once in a back number of 'Pravda' an obituary notice of Dzerzhinsky, the founder of the Cheka and first head of the GPU, written by his successor. It described Dzerzhinsky as a saint, an ascetic, a man who rose above petty bourgeois emotions like pity, or a respect for justice or for human life; a man of infinite industry; a rare spirit whose revolutionary passion was unearthly and uncontaminated. The very prose of the obituary notice was lyrical. It had a rhythm like a religious chant. I thought, and still think, that I had found in it the quintessence of revolution; and I hated this quintessence because it was a denial of everything that has been gained in the slow, painful progress of civilisation; because it was beastly, because it idealised and spiritualised evil; because it glorified destruction and death; and, going beneath the animal, beneath hate, beneath lust, beneath every kind of appetite, founded itself on impulses which, though they have in the past sometimes been organised into abominable, underground cults, have never before held sway over a hundred and sixty million people inhabiting a sixth of the world's surface.

This is the Terror. The people who execute it are naturally not normal. Most of them are not Russians. I counted in the Presiduum of the GPU only two unquestionably Russian names. The present acting head is a Polish Jew. A good number of the underlings are also Jews, with a fair sprinkling of Letts and Poles. The 'flaming sword of the proletariat' has been forged in ghettoes and wherever are collected men with a grudge against their fellows and against society; and the population of Russia lives, terrified, under its shadow. It is a product of pogroms, and is itself the greatest pogrom of history. To attempt to make its acts or its procedure conform with a civilised judicial system, as did certain politicians and newspapers in connection with the recent Metropolitan-Vickers affair – to judge them on that basis is like trying to read military strategy into the frenzied movements of a frightened tiger, or, better, to extract enlightened moral principles from the ravings of a diseased mind.

The theory of the class war has provided the GPU with an instrument after its own heart, the class enemy is anyone, and it is the business of the GPU to destroy the class enemy. Since the class war cannot end until the dictatorship of the proletariat has 'liquidated' itself – that is, never – it offers the GPU a prospect of unending activity. Priests and relics of the old Tsarist bourgeoisie, even kulaks, have become *vieux jeu* when the whole peasantry is available, and when, thanks to the passport system, the town populations have been delivered into its hands.

The GPU is responsible for defining class enemies, for sentencing them, and for executing the sentence. It decides that a Ukrainian peasant who has hidden a few poods of grain in his house to feed himself and his family through the winter when everything else has been requisitioned by the Government, is a class enemy, and, accordingly, either shoots or exiles him. It has spies everywhere, listening, watching; every so often it unearths or invents – scarcely, I believe, itself knowing which – a counter-revolutionary plot, and, by torture and threats and bribery, gathers the material for a spectacular State trial. Like some criminals, it has a morbid appetite for publicity, and loves to figure on the front page in foreign newspapers; like all diseased minds, it is morbidly curious about everyone and everything, and makes a speciality of using for its purposes facts about the private lives of people who have fallen into its hands or whom it wishes for any reason to terrorise. The weak are its particular prey; and it is able, even without violence, even without their knowing how it has happened, to reduce them to a condition in which they will confess anything, promise anything.

Bolsheviks justify the class war on the ground that it is necessary in order to achieve a state of classlessness. Actually, however, its directors have evolved into a ruling class more privileged and more powerful than any other in the world; a ruling class that has power of life and death over the whole population, that is utterly irresponsible in the exercise of its privileges, that is beyond criticism because to criticise it is to criticise the dictatorship of the proletariat, which means to be guilty of treason against the Soviet State and to qualify for the death sentence. While social inequalities are being ruthlessly smoothed out at one end of society, new and more arbitrary and more pronounced inequalities are coming into existence at the other. Each layer of class enemies that is destroyed reveals another whose destruction is necessary.

This is worse than civil war. It is a people making war on itself. It is war by the proletariat for the proletariat on the proletariat. It is the dictatorship of the proletariat blockading the dictatorship of the proletariat. In consequence of this class war, Russia has become a battlefield and the Russians a subject people. As the productivity of these subject people and of this battlefield becomes more and more inadequate, the Soviet Government calls for more and more frenzied activity on the 'class war front' – a vicious circle which seems to bear out Danton's gloomy prophecy – made when, having sent many to the guillotine, he realised that he would shortly find his way there himself – that revolutions, after they have consumed everyone else, at last consume themselves.

‡══‡

3

THE KINGDOM OF HEAVEN ON EARTH

The Kingdom of Heaven on Earth has haunted this Generation, as the Evangelical's Hell haunted our fathers, but much more disastrously, since eternal torment at least pre-supposes eternal life – that is, Eternity and sin – that is, imperfection; whereas the Kingdom of Heaven on Earth is all pretence, a denial of the very nature of life. If an epitaph were required for this sad and terrible time, it might well be found in 'The Kingdom of Heaven on Earth'.

The basic error is to suppose that under any circumstances there might be a perfect State, since the very existence of a State at all is a symptom of imperfection; or, under any circumstances a perfect law, since Law exists only because Man is imperfect, sinful, because of the Fall. Heaven and Hell are conceivable, but the Kingdom of Heaven on Earth is inconceivable. Otherwise, it would have come to pass long ago, and there have been no occasion for Satan to tempt Christ by showing him the Kingdoms of the Earth or for Christ to reject them. Otherwise, Christ would have lived instead of dying, and the long, troubled history of mankind be shorn of its horror and its glory.

What does it mean, a Kingdom of Heaven on Earth? It means that it would be possible so to arrange matters that there would be no injustice, no exploitation, no conflict, no having of our reward according as we pursue power or lust or love; it means that Man, imperfect Man, could create a perfect environment, and therefore that there is nothing in the universe greater than Man, no God, and nothing in living on this earth for a few years except living on this earth for a few years; it means that religion, art, all the obscure longings which from age to age, from civilization to civilization, have led individuals to reach beyond the bounds of Flesh and Time, have been a vain delusion.

That is Hell if you like, the materialist's hell or doom, the most frightful which has ever been envisaged. It would be a fascinating, though sombre, pursuit to trace this idea from its origins, and through all its manifold phases – whether in terms of scientific marvels like those HG Wells envisaged, or of social felicity such as the Fabians and Marxists and all their many affiliates have long proclaimed, or of mere asinine sensual well-being such as Walt Whitman, DH Lawrence and others pointed to as the fulfilment of life. Materialism is the soil in which it has grown; first a little, tender shoot - education which was to perfect the mind, science which was to perfect the body and its circumstances, original goodness in these favourable conditions blossoming, and everyone healthy, wealthy and wise for ever and ever.

The little, tender shoot did not fulfil its promise, but ripened into an alarming crop. Many became literate, yes; but what did they read? Wealth accumulated, yes; but how was it spent and how distributed? Original goodness blossomed, yes; but its manifestations were indistinguishable from the manifestations of original sin, except that they were unbridled, unashamed, arrogant. The confidently announced Kingdom of Heaven on Earth, in fact, failed to put in an appearance. Instead, there was the most ferocious war in history; poverty and misery and suffering without end.

What was now to be done? God and the Kingdom of Heaven Within had been abolished to prepare for the coming of a Kingdom of Heaven Without, which had not materialised; but something still remained - hatred, greed, fear, all the terrible passions which flesh is heir to. These remained, and might be mobilised, first to achieve power, then, having achieved it, as an instrument of Terror. Preach hatred, not just for the purpose of waging a war, but as an everlasting gospel, a means of bringing to pass the Kingdom of Heaven on Earth!

Insist, that instead of it being possible for the strong and the weak, the wise and the foolish, the crippled and the whole-of-limb, the sick and the healthy, to live peaceably together because they are brothers, having one father, God, the only possibility is for the strong utterly to destroy the weak - one class, the proletariat, destroying all others; one race, the German, triumphing over all others. Call the result, whatever it may be, the Kingdom of Heaven on Earth; lie and lie and lie to persuade that it really is so and whoever refuses at any rate to pretend to be convinced, kill.

4

NAZI TERROR

Terrorism has been an invariable accompaniment of Nazi rule, whether in Germany or in those territories which have been, by subterfuge or force of arms, brought under German domination. As its name implies, it is the promotion of a state of blind unreasoning fear.

The basis of all civilization is the codification of law; the community's moral sense finds expression in laws, and though their observance is based in the last resort on fear of the consequences of contravening them, such fear, being dependent on a known contingency, is inoffensive, mild, with no nightmarish quality in it.

Terrorism, the negation of law, aims at creating an enduring state of fear, not of particular consequences of particular acts, but nameless, like a child's fear in the dark. Only by means of terrorism was it possible for Nazi rule to be established. Law implies the application of reason to human affairs, to judicial settlement of disputes, the possibility of different point of view whose validity must be carefully weighed. Such conceptions are abhorrent to those whose leader has laid down the principle that truth must not be investigated objectively, but only its favourable aspects presented. Law had to be destroyed and replaced by terrorism.

Where law reigns, a knock at the front door at night will not unduly disturb those within; if they are law-abiding, they need not dread police visitations, and they have sufficient confidence in the establishment of public order to be unafraid of private molestation.

When terrorism reigns, any household, however blameless, will be thrown into a state of perturbation by an unknown visitor who comes at night. That their consciences are clear provides no guarantee that they may not have deserved punishment, others as innocent as themselves, they know, have been taken away, and it may now be their turn. In such circumstances, the authorities are more like tribal Gods, unaccountable in their rage, requiring to be propitiated, than an expression of the general will to be orderly and secure.

It is difficult for those who have grown up in an orderly society whose structure they take for granted, to imagine themselves subjected to terrorism. The edifice of a law seems so firmly constructed, their individual rights so securely established, that they cannot envisage a state of lawlessness in which there are no individual rights whatsoever, and the whole population is reduced to a condition of servitude.

So ordinary Germans felt before 1933. Even Hitler then protested his respect for constitutional procedure, and a Nazi dictatorship seemed inconceivable. When Hitler actually became Chancellor, still it was thought, within Germany and without, that Civil Law, institutions like the Supreme Court, the Roman Catholic and Protestant Churches, were beyond his reach.

This was to leave terrorism out of account. Almost Hitler's first act as head of State was to institute the Gestapo, the secret police, on the pattern of the Soviet Ogpu. By means of the Gestapo, it was possible to frighten everyone, and to make them, being frightened, subservient. Unorthodoxy, that is, not being an ostentatiously zealous National Socialist, became a crime deserving of punishment; and the said Gestapo was responsible for arresting whoever was, or might be, guilty of this crime, sentencing him and executing the sentence.

In effect, the whole population was delivered into the Gestapo's hands. Against anyone a criminal charge might plausibly be preferred, since anyone was liable to have expressed or thought some opinion critical of the Government. Safety, if at all attainable, lay in expressing no opinions at all, in not even thinking just echoing officially provided slogans loudly and earnestly. It was as though the whole population had been arrested and provisionally released, instead of, as where there is a law, arrests being provisional until guilt has been proved. Everyone was in the position of prisoners on remand, and liable at any moment to be brought for trial on an unspecified charge.

Is it wonderful, then, that they were meek and servile? A conversation casually entered into might betray some trifling unorthodoxy, and mean being swallowed up in a concentration camp; professional advancement, livelihood, depended on not being suspected of anti-Nazi sentiments, and personalities, of family and of friendship, provided a means of oppression. The duty of spying on one another was assiduously preached, and the child who reported his father's lack of zeal was held up to admiration. Laughter was highly dangerous, and a neglected or carelessly muttered 'Heil Hitler' was a serious misdemeanour.

By such means it is possible for an unscrupulous and ruthless minority to impose its dictatorship on the majority; to make them obedient, apparently amenable to any policy, however violent and inconsistent, and to inculcate them with any doctrine, however unreasonable and absurd. Unity of purpose is achieved, but by imposition from without, not by conviction from within. It is the unity of the chain-gang. In the process of achieving this chain-gang unity, whatever differentiates a civilised community from its jungle origins is lost.

There can be no trust between man and man when all are in duty bound to act as informers; there can be no intellectual or moral integrity when opinions are dictated and any deviation from them punished; there can be no learning or art, no pursuit of truth at all, when the free exercise of curiosity and speculation is made a crime. Human life, so confined, is something very paltry, lacking in dignity, insignificant. Whatever is fine and permanent in human achievement has been realised through individuals courageously facing the circumstances of their being; and a society is civilised to the extent to which it makes this possible. Terrorism, which aims at putting out the spiritual light, is the antithesis of civilisation.

The atmosphere it creates is one of omnipresent fear; the personnel it relies on must inevitably be the most cruel and odious members of the community, since only those will undertake the task of deliberately, systematically, terrifying their fellows. Himmler, head of the Gestapo, has become this type of terrorist, moving secretly and acting suddenly, always dreaded. When new territory is occupied, he is the first to arrive on the scene and with his arrival, the reign of terrorism begins, another devastated area is created.

All who have ever given evidence of a capacity for independent thought must flee or hide themselves; what was formerly considered virtue becomes vice, and things which were abhorrent, are exalted. As punishment for no evident reason is more productive of fear than punishment for a stated cause, the terrorist gives no explanation of his seizures. Laws, even when they are unjust, are at least formulated, and immunity may be achieved by observing them; without formulated laws, there can be no immunity for anyone. The machinery for enforcing the observance of laws exists, but the laws which are to be enforced, are not defined. Coercion is unaccountable, and therefore universally and constantly dreaded.

This is Tyranny in its most extreme form. Even absolute monarchs were held accountable to God, but terrorism requires no earthly or heavenly sanction. It is power, naked and unbridled; relentless as a forest fire, which as it sweeps along, destroys everything and everyone.

+>——=+

5

THE PHONEY WAR

O n a bright September Sunday, when the church congregations at morning service had barely emerged, in
accents of quavering ferocity Mr. Neville Chamberlain announced that another war had begun. Almost immediately
afterwards the sirens sounded, and into the blue sky, with one
accord, rose the captive balloons. It seemed that the moment
of ecstatic destruction had come. The prophecy was to be
fulfilled, a great bonfire to be made. Civilization was to be
destroyed; a dreaded, but still longed-for, calamity was about
to come to pass. All the despair, all the bewilderment, all the
unreal hopes and unmeant resolution of years were to find
now an ultimate fulfilment in death and destruction raining
from the skies. There was a pause, like the period of stillness
before a tropical storm breaks; the little silence, which pre-
cedes, alike, the ecstasy of life and of death. Everyone waited
– and nothing happened.

Every circumstance of war existed, except war. Forces had
been mobilised, air-raid precautions organised, black-out imposed, hospital beds cleared, even cardboard coffins prepared
for the dead. Well-meaning ladies presented themselves to

organise canteens, including some, now ancient, associated with similar enterprises in the past; in the War Office there was a frenzy of activity, and at recruiting offices queues formed. About the dark streets traffic moved cautiously; theatres, cinemas, and other places of amusement closed their doors, and from Broadcasting House came an incessant stream of news, exhortations and solemnity. In the lately completed London University building in Bloomsbury, a vast, miscellaneous company assembled with the general object of informing and enlightening.

With great secrecy, and ancient and largely obsolete equipment, a British Expeditionary Force was assembled to proceed to France. It duly proceeded there, without, as was proudly claimed, the loss of a single life. Like a revived performance after a long interval of a once successful play, properties, costumes, make-up, were brought out of the boxes in which they had been stored away, and lines learnt long ago remembered and spoken again. If the production proceeded somewhat haltingly and laboriously, it still proceeded – leading lady no longer youthful, haggard in the limelight, and the chorus as they kicked their legs in the air less nimble than when the show was first put on a quarter of a century before. Though, however, the actors still could be made up to give a plausible representation of their former roles, still could speak their lines with some conviction, the attention of the audience showed signs of wandering. Somehow, something was wrong.

There was a lack of relation between what was being said and done and what was happening – or rather not happening. Breeches and polished boots which made their way at lunchtime from the War Office to clubs in Pall Mall, belonged to another setting; their wearers accoutred for some other war – lean and somewhat woeful faces, occasionally with monocles, surveying a scene which they found puzzling [yet] scarcely knew why. Mahogany naval visages likewise seemingly bewildered; and characters emerging from the Treasury, umbrella on arm, somehow lost looking, as they gazed down Whitehall at Big Ben, and up at Nelson's column; seemingly relieved to find these two familiar landmarks still extant. Everything was proceeding according to plan, and yet a doubt obstinately remained.

The absence of action evoked in some breasts the hope that the war, which never was to happen, and ostensibly had happened, might, after all, never happen. It seemed so extraordinary, when such sudden devastation had been prophesied, that, in fact, there should be neither death nor destruction; a state of war but no warfare. Perhaps even now, despite all that had been said and done, it was only a crisis, like other past crises, and would pass. Perhaps, as before, there would be negotiations, moments of tension, and then order-papers waved in Parliament; late editions spreading the good news – another and a greater Munich. A few desultory bursts of artillery fire on the Western Front, an exchange of decorations by Allied commanders, other such harmless undertakings – all this amounted to very little more than, in an attempt at seduction, an arm thrown round the back of a chair which might have rested there naturally; no more than a shifting of position, which could be due to mere restlessness. Surely with so tame a beginning, many secretly felt, the immense catastrophe about which so many warnings had been delivered might yet be averted.

Buildings were still securely standing, traffic still circulated, restaurants still served meals, and money still bought what shops still offered for sale. There might, as far as could be seen, have been no declaration of war, no abortive air-raid warning, no ecstatic expectation that the hour of doom had come. In Downing Street, still Prime Minister, sat Mr. Chamberlain, who had brought back peace with honour so short a time before; in Westminster still deliberated the same Parliament which had risen almost as one man to signalise their joy in the Munich Agreement. Where an end had been expected, there was not even a beginning. There was nothing. Everything was as it had always been - or so it seemed.

This reluctance of the war to come to pass, although officially it was being waged, caused some irritation, particularly in the United States. Senator Borah spoke contemptuously of a 'phoney war', and the phrase took on. American newspaper correspondents who had come to Europe in the full expectation of being able to cover themselves with glory by their descriptions of the bloody struggle which had been engaged, were disappointed and indignant when they found there was nothing to describe. They and their European colleagues, if no one else, found the phoney war dispiriting. They had the greatest difficulty in procuring any material at all for their despatches, and fell back on describing the boredom of their own lives at GHQ. With great difficulty they managed to make something out of conducted tours of an inactive front, and of visits to a Maginot Line, splendidly equipped with lifts, running water, cinemas, and even bordellos. The French Army, they reported, was in magnificent heart, and being provided with no less than a litre of red wine per day; British troops were displaying all their usual humorous gallantry and endurance, and the standard examples were given of cockney and other humour – "Arf a mo' 'Itler,' Bruce Bairnsfather's Old Bill called back to active service along with other of his contemporaries, high and low, including Ian Hay, who presided over the Public Relations branch of the War Office, the First Hundred Thousand in this war being in words, not men.

It was not only in Senator Borah's heart, however, that a doubt existed. Others, who could not, or would not, put their doubts into words, felt a similar uneasiness. The appearance of things bore no relation to what was really happening – like an old love affair after an interval of twenty years or so; the same endearments used, the same restaurant visited, the same wine drunk, and then, in a sudden ghastly glare of light, the realisation that faces had become gaunt and haggard, flesh withered, hair grizzled, and desire all spent.

Those set in authority over us achieve such a position by virtue of a certain aptness, or suitability, in them, however little they may seem to deserve their eminence, or however large a part chicanery or violence may have seemed to play in its attainment. The most absolute dictator and the most democratically elected prime minister or president alike exercise power over their fellows in the last resort only because they represent them – collective emotions and fears stirring in their individual breasts, collective words spoken by their individual mouths. A Laval or a Hitler or a Roosevelt, a Mr. Attlee even, all, to a greater or smaller extent, satisfy this condition. Chance may wash them into eminence, but their fitness to be eminent at a particular time and in particular circumstances keeps them there.

Out of the collectivity crystallizes, by whatever procedure, its master or masters. This crystallization may be achieved by means of violence, or trickery, or even mere bribery, but it can only survive for any length of time in so far as there is a valid relation between the leaders and the led. Authority rises from below, however circumlocutory the route. There is no such thing as 'irresponsible authority', except briefly. Chinless, impotent Maharajah may stay put on his throne for a year or so; much married, distracted heiress may continue for a little while to command obedience, but in the long run both are alike doomed because the current which must flow between those who exert power and those upon whom it is exerted has been short circuited.

Thus, from the led the leaders may be deduced, and vice versa. In England there was Neville Chamberlain, former sisal grower and mayor of Birmingham, whose moment of glory had come when he returned from Munich bearing Hitler's promissory note of peace with honour to the great and noisy delight of his assembled countrymen. Since that triumphant occasion his fortunes had steadily and badly declined. From peace with honour he had been irresistibly projected into war with dishonour. His naive trust in the word of dictators had turned into senile fury at their perfidy. Like Lear, he declaimed in quavering accents his determination to make them rue their bad faith – he would do such things, what they were yet he knew not. Into the future he could not see, but out of the past, to stiffen his dwindling authority, he garnered the solid shape of Mr. Churchill to be his First Lord of the Admiralty.

Mr. Churchill belonged to an earlier mould. The nineteenth century had been skipped altogether in his makeup. He derived from an earlier form of society altogether. Perhaps because of his American ancestry, he was able to dress up, behave, speak, and, it may be, even to feel as though no Gladstone or Disraeli, not to mention Lloyd George, Bonar Law, Baldwin or Ramsay MacDonald, had interposed themselves between himself and Chatham. Like one of those stage coaches brought out to celebrate a Dickens anniversary, with horns blowing and horses careering along the motorized Strand, this remarkable man, in the mood of his ancestor Marlborough and the diction of Macaulay, made ready to save his country from disaster. The massive strength of the nineteenth century was reduced to only a poor whimper of fatuous gullibility and benevolence, but, by a curious chance, an earlier England, seemingly long passed away, suddenly and surprisingly manifested itself with quite remarkable effect, if in a somewhat vulgarised or Hollywood version.

If Mr. Churchill, as First Lord, brought Mr. Chamberlain's Cabinet a sorely needed touch of colour, Mr. Anthony Eden endowed it with whatever remained of the credit which had accrued to him as a Conservative Foreign Minister who had resigned, rather than continue to countenance, a policy of appeasing the axis. The bloom of those days when he first declaimed so earnestly in favour of peace at Geneva and Westminster was somewhat faded; those journeyings from capital to capital in the same pursuit, when, with finger tips pressed together, he listened attentively to what Stalin or Tatarescu or Goering had to say, seemed now a remote, and perhaps unsubstantial, enterprise. Even so, his presence in the Cabinet added to its repute, and created the feeling that youth was being given a chance. Age could not wither him, nor custom stale his infinite banality.

The others were all familiar faces – Sir Kingsley Wood, Mr Hore-Belisha, M. Walter Elliot, Sir John Simon. They were still theoretically a National Government, first assembled under the auspices of Ramsay MacDonald to execute a doctor's mandate, and now retaining faint vestigial remains, in Mr Harold Nicolson and others, of National Labour, and of several Liberal varieties, ever ready to sink party differences and take office. Between the wars, with only brief interruptions, they had governed, but their reign was drawing to its close, and most of them would soon be little heard of except to be denounced as Guilty Men. The impression they made as they directed what came to be known, somewhat inaptly, as the war effort, was rather of weariness or decrepitude than guilt. A quality of twilight was in their faces and voices as they appealed to their countrymen to 'Save for the Brave,' not adding, however, that none but the brave deserved to save; as they assembled together or dispersed, making speeches, thumbing through documents, taking their places in Parliament, in the Carlton Club; spreading out their already abbreviated Times or Daily Telegraph in the morning, and somnolently listening to the nine o'clock news at night.

In France there was no such figure as Mr Churchill to turn to. Instead, an aged Marshal was preparing to surrender, and the last poor pillars of the Third Republic, shaking and tottering, would provide no impediment. Daladier, Reynaud, Leon Blum, Chautemps, Flandin and others, who for a quarter of a century past had been in and out of Ministries, felt their power ebbing away. Photographed in groups with various combinations and permutations, delivering orations, saving the franc only to lose it again, Right, Left and Centre - now it seemed they had little or nothing to offer, or even to suggest. Even more than their prototypes across the Channel, they had become quite irrelevant. Other forces were shaping which would sweep them relentlessly aside.

Already the most hopeful direction in which to look was westward - old dry parent trunk hoping for sap to drain back into its parched tissue from distant shoots still apparently green and alive. Such hopes were not in vain. In the White House president Roosevelt, preparing to win his third presidential election on a promise to keep America out of the war, was also, at the same time, preparing to take her in fine style into it. His extraordinary political knockabout performance had now gone on for eight years, and his position seemed stronger than ever. Seldom, if ever, has such sustained political agility been seen. His followers and his associates might change, sometimes with startling suddenness, but he went marching on.

Since his death, attempts have been made to deduce a consistent pattern out of his conduct of American affairs, to trace through them some consistent purpose which was being pursued; but the more his career is examined, the more inconsequential and, at the same time, fabulous, does it appear. He played by ear rather than following any score of his own or another's composition; he improvised, he smiled - he and his consort ever, ever smiling. Having got into the White House, there he triumphantly remained, to the almost apoplectic rage of his opponents, and the delight of his varied supporters, all

of whom were persuaded to believe that he was deeply concerned with their particular interests – Southern Democrats
convinced that though he might for political reasons pay lip
service to ideas like racial equality, White supremacy was safe
in his hands (as, indeed, it was); Left Wing intellectuals equally
convinced that though he might, for political reasons, associate with reactionary Southern Democrats, his heart was on
the Left, and all his endeavours directed towards improving
the circumstances of what he called, in the jargon his regime
brought into current usage, the 'under privileged;' farmers,
trade unionists, cranks of every sort and description, all likewise convinced that in Roosevelt they had a faithful friend
and champion.

If the Western democracies were looking westwards, he was
looking eastwards, knowing that there he, too, had a role to
play, and that a major one. Already he had issued appeals to all
the Governments of all the world, and would be frequently
addressing this large, but nebulous, clientele, later expanded
into all the people everywhere. Mr Sumner Welles and other
emissaries had made the rounds from capital to capital, vo-
luminously reporting, but leaving little trace behind of their
wanderings; and an intimate correspondence had begun between the President and Mr Churchill in the guise of a 'Naval
Person.' In his wheel chair, cigarette in long holder tilted into
the air, heavy metal braces which, in his last public utterance,
he for the first time complained were heavy to carry around
with him – thus accoutred, Roosevelt, too, was anxious and
ready to enter the fray.

On the other side were the dictators – the Axis or anti-
Comintern contingent, which had acquired, as a temporary

associate, the Comintern. Hitler and Mussolini were then seemingly at the top of their bent. The Führer's somnambulistic course had almost reached its stupendous climax. Now, when its ignominious end is known, it is difficult to remember the days of his glory. Yet how tremendous they were! What a concentration of purpose his single purpose generated – outward and visible in those howls of animal approval which punctuated his speeches, and became a familiar, if horrifying, sound even in English ears. His phosphorescent personality, physically so horrifying, yet succeeded in imposing itself on the German people, and in producing a kind of fascination, or, at any rate, obsession, elsewhere. Afterwards, notably at Nuremberg, his associates tried to show that their acceptance of his will's finality was hesitant, or positively reluctant. Their excuses, however, were unconvincing even to themselves. They followed him with blind confidence. He was their Pied Piper, whose words lured them on. If the end was destruction, his as well as theirs, their faith never faltered. In his star they could not but believe. Everything seemed to be working in his favour; and perhaps even the destructive end was what, in their hearts, they longed for – a stupendous bonfire of themselves and their world, a collective act of suttee or self-immolation whose like had never before been seen.

The junior partner, Mussolini, was now set on the same course, though after doubts and hesitations, which still occasionally recurred. Like Lancelot Gobbo, there was a fiend who said 'On!' and an inner voice which urged him 'Back!' On the whole, the fiend had it, though the final step had still to be taken. The Duce hesitated on the brink of war, anxious to plunge in, but fearful that the water might be chilly, occasionally inserting a toe to test its temperature, taking up a position on the diving board for a decisive plunge, and then deciding still to wait a little longer. If only his Italians had been Germans! – but they remained irretrievably Italian even when he made them goose-step, and actually toyed with the idea of planting forests in the north of Italy in the expectation that, by thus altering geographical conditions, he might pro- duce a more warlike people suitable to execute his purposes. On the one hand he saw a prospect of illimitable loot; and on the other, some native prudence, which had survived his later megalomania made him hesitate.

He lived in a state of perpetual irresolution, of irritation with himself and with everyone else – particularly with his minute King, Victor Emmanuel, whom he had kept on the throne of Italy, and from whom he received constant little pricks and annoyances. He wanted to be absolutely sure that victory would come to him without the necessity of winning it on the field of battle. His envy and dislike of Hitler warred with his conviction that the Führer's star would never wane. Like Macbeth, he continually assured himself that Burnham Wood could never walk to Dunsinane – and yet it might; no man of woman born could interrupt the Führer's triumphant course – and yet who knew if there might not be one, like Macduff, from his mother's womb untimely ripped? For Mus- solini, these were uneasy months, full of hesitation, changes of mood, stomach disorders, and the exhausting blisses of a youthful mistress.

Far away in the Kremlin, inscrutable and watchful, Hitler's latest colleague, Stalin, took quiet advantage of opportunities as they presented themselves. To the Duce's annoyance, he had pulled in quicker and bigger dividends than the earlier members of the Axis firm. By his sudden reversal of policy he had been able to gather up half Poland and the Baltic States, and, though he found himself for the time being engaged in an unexpectedly stubborn conflict with Finland, might be expected to make other gains before very long. From remote Georgia he had obscurely appeared as one of Lenin's minor lieutenants, and since that time, with ruthless and patient persistence, he had become, in himself, the dictatorship of the proletariat by the simple expedient of eliminating all other actual and potential claimants to that important position.

For the moment, relations between Berlin and Moscow seemed most harmonious. Friendly and congratulatory messages were exchanged, and the German Foreign Minister, von Ribbentrop, could wear on his breast the Order of Lenin designed to honour the greatest heroes in the struggle for world proletarian revolution. War supplies, which had been promised in the Russo-German Agreement of August 1939, were being punctually delivered, and other conversations were pending designed to extend the basis of collaboration in return for further participation in Hitler's bounty. Aryan superman and proletarian dictatorship seemed to have joined forces, and to represent a mighty combination, capable of dividing the world between them.

‡══‡

6

LETTERS FROM AMERICA

April 21, 1946.

New York

Dearest Kit, I'm leaving New York for Washington tomorrow, and send you a note before I go. Wandering about a town with nothing much to do is a rather melancholy occupation. This is what I've been doing over Easter. Yesterday, Easter Sunday, there was a huge fashion parade in Fifth Avenue - masses of well-dressed and well-fed people aimlessly drifting to and fro in bright sunshine. After all the desolation of Europe, it was in a way impressive, and yet I don't know. I didn't envy them particularly, or feel any greater confidence in their future than in that of their shabby, hungry equivalents in Paris or London. The skull beneath the flesh I always seem to see. Perhaps morbidly, and have too keen a nose for mortality.

April 24, 1946.

Washington

I was delighted and relieved to find here a batch of letters from you and the children and to know that all was well.

Hughie quoted to me some lines of verse last time I saw him which finished up, 'For terrible is earth.' I've said this line over and over to myself – terrible when one's alone, especially after a certain age. There's so little one wants now, and that little so precious in consequence; just to be with the faces one knows and cares for, and to hear unfamiliar voices; no more. I have an awful feeling when I wake up in the night that I made one of the great mistakes of my life when I didn't just settle down and write on leaving the army. However, I didn't, and no doubt it'll turn out for the best. Certainly, if writing 'The Forties' is to be considered worth doing, I couldn't have chosen a better method of equipping myself for it.

29 April, 1946.

Washington

I'm staying for the time being in a faded antique flat in the house of an aged Frenchwoman. There's no cuppa on the premises, so I have to get up and go out to a drug store for my morning coffee. Everyone does this, seated on tall stools at a counter. Then I acquire two enormous newspapers through whose stagnant columns I swim lazily for an hour or so. After that there are press conferences, visits to the Senate, etc etc.

How unutterably contemptible is power and all its uses. I've seen so much of it, too much. How loathsome are legislative assemblies and political gatherings of all sorts and descriptions. Strident men getting up and asserting their opinions, straining to establish their authority. I can't imagine myself going on doing this – I mean to the extent of conveying their importance, an instrument in their struggle for power. As far as I'm concerned, let them keep their power and good luck to them. I don't want any of it. I need scarcely say that I haven't done any writing to speak of, and wonder now if I ever shall.

May 21, 1946.

Washington

I've just emerged from one of the longest and most unrelieved fits of melancholia I've ever experienced in which dark thoughts or devils quite possessed me. Perhaps it was a change of life or something. It went on all through the journey and in New York and here – a sense of such desolation that the very air I breathed seemed full of corruption. I've only just now begun to work at all, and though I wouldn't say I was even now particularly cheerful I can get along. Journalism is a loathsome occupation but I suppose I deserve it. There's a wonderful passage in Coleridge, which seems to me the cri du coeur of all journalists in which he says that like an ostrich he's planted too many eggs in the hot sand of the desert of this world.

May 28, 1946.

Washington

I've taken over in the office here. It's a bit heavy going to begin with but I suppose one'll get used to it in time. I really think that this job will just about cure me of what Hughie calls my realpolitik. On Saturday I went to a joint session of the Congress and Truman came in and there was a lot of excitement. Poor little man – he seemed very lost. How absurd a thing is power, especially when combined with insignificance. At least it's more pitiable in such circumstances. I suppose ceremonial and all that has to be invented to help it out. King George VI is a more satisfactory proposition than President Truman. I'm haunted by the idea of not getting any of my own work done, by those terrible Ciano sheets, by this sense of time slipping past. And yet I don't know that it matters much. It's only one's egotism which makes one think it matters. My morning cuppa has at last been organised (made by myself which I really prefer) and I've found a swimming pool in a club here so get my favourite exercise, and altogether it's not so bad except that I'm so unutterably sick of newspapers and find America a lonely desolate sort of place.

16 June, 1946.

Washington

The weeks pass by quickly now. I've got into a routine, my usual - up at seven and make the cuppa and potter around in a dressing gown; then newspapers and picking over the dungheap of this world's affairs for my little necessary morsels; then my own little shovelful or two into the heap; then the evening and a stroll; then a glass or two and some talk if any available. I do actually now occasionally write a little on my own. A routine is essential when one becomes older, a framework or scaffolding to hold up one's tottering life.

America as I'm sure you'll find, is a place about which one has highly varied feelings. One doesn't acquire a settled relationship with the place. Sometimes it seems utterly abhorrent and at other times oddly sympathetic, I suppose according to one's own mood.

September 2, 1946.

Washington

How infinitely melancholy the affairs of the world are just now. I can't tell you with what weariness I approach the task of having my little daily say about them from here. Then every now and again, perhaps walking in the morning, I suddenly forget all about them and feel briefly the mystery of things and am suddenly serene.

August 20, 1947.

Washington

The Regents Park flat sounds absolutely wonderful and in the circumstances I'd personally make any financial sacrifice to get somewhere more or less agreeable to live. It seems to me that's the thing to go for. Present intentions are that I should leave for Tokyo at the end of September and be back in London late November. Then I shall never go on any more travels unless we decide to emigrate all together to give the boys a better chance elsewhere. As it's turned out I've scarcely been able to go to New York at all. I only spent one rather ghastly weekend there with the Broughs who now live in a remote suburb with a car and a flavour of death.

November 15, 1947

Los Angeles

On Monday I go to Seattle and early Tuesday fly to Tokyo via Alaska. You may be sure I shan't linger unnecessarily on the way. I feel as though the day I walk into 5 Cambridge Gate and am home at last with us all under one roof will be the happiest day of all my life. This place, Los Angeles, is ugly and rather ludicrous but I'm quite glad to have seen it. The drive across has made me feel well after being rather run down at the end of my time in Washington and I feel full of ideas about writing and everything else.

My darling although actually I'll be further away in Tokyo than in Washington I feel nearer every day because I'm on my way back.

All my love as always,
Malcolm

7

FELLOW TRAVELLERS

M r. Adolphe Menjou the other day expressed astonish-ment that so many rich men should be Communists or fellow travellers. It seemed to him an extraordinary cir-cumstance that a millionaire should embrace a creed which, if it succeeded, could not but deprive him of the advantag-es of his wealth. As a matter of fact, so complex a thing is human nature, there are plenty of precedents for such ap-parent illogicality. For instance, Talleyrand, an aristocrat and a bishop, associated himself with an anti-clerical revolutionary movement, and Nietzsche, prophet of the Aryan superman, personally disliked Germans, and spent most of his life out-side Germany, dying at last in a lunatic asylum. There have been Jewish anti-Semites, and male feminists, and brewers who were total abolitionists. The fact is that human behav-iour cannot be comprehended in the concept of enlightened self-interest.

Men are as liable to pursue their own ruin as their own ad-vantage. In Hitler's day Nazi processions sometimes included a little melancholy contingent of opponents or victims of the regime displaying the slogan 'Down with us!' Those who marched behind this sad placard were Nazi fellow-travellers. Their slogan defines both the mood and the destination of all fellow-travelling.

If, however, it has often been the case that human beings have passionately advocated causes which cannot but encompass their own ultimate destruction, an historian in the future, trying to piece together the pattern of this strange time will surely still be interested and puzzled by the motivation of contemporary fellow-travellers. These millionaires, he will ask himself, who identified themselves with forces unmistakeably destructive of their wealth; these pious clergymen who lent themselves to propaganda which made a mockery of the faith they professed; these admirable scholars who contentedly swallowed the most monstrous perversions of historical scholarship – what exactly were they after?

In retrospect, the spectacle of professed democrats exulting over the multiplication of Police States, and of internationalists applauding each new triumph of Slav nationalism, will inevitably seem rather extraordinary. However inured to the vagaries of human nature, eyebrows are likely still to be raised at the record of earnest progressives railing against any infringement of civil liberties at home and rejoicing over the arbitrary judgments of People's Courts abroad; over gentle humanitarians who find the death penalty imposed for crimes of violence brutal and unnecessary, but who so readily overlook brutality and coercion on a vast scale when it is sponsored by the Kremlin.

Seeking enlightenment, our historian may well turn to the vast and often turgid literature of Soviet adulation. If so, he is unlikely to derive much benefit therefrom. Turning over the pages of, for instance, the Webbs' 'Soviet Communism: A New Civilisation', or of The Dean of Canterbury's 'The Socialist Sixth of the World', would but add to his bewilderment. Did not the Webbs, he would ask himself, devote much of their life and endeavours to improving social conditions? How, then, were they able to tolerate the admitted fact of large numbers of Russian citizens in forced labour camps? Were they not earnest believers in democratic institutions? How, then, when they prided themselves on their exactness and moderation, could they have reached the asinine conclusion that 'the USSR is the most inclusive and equalised democracy in the world'? Was not the phrase 'inevitability of gradualness' actually coined by the Webbs? How, then, did they come so to admire the Kremlin's most ungradual procedure? Was not the Dean of Canterbury a strong advocate of humane practices? How, then, did he so readily turn a blind eye on the activities of the Russian political police, and so readily accept the results of obviously fraudulent elections in Russia and Russia's satellite states?

Such questions would scarcely be elucidated by a study of the authorised Communist scriptures. These are full of exhortations to violence and conflict. There is little gradualness to be found in them. They bear about as close a relation to the Thirty-nine Articles as Hitler's 'Mein Kampf' does to the Sermon on the Mount. Between the Lubianka prison and a Fabian Summer School there is set a chasm which would seem impassable, except that ideological athletes like Mr Bernard Shaw have been able to leap nimbly across it.

Again, the Communist Party Line has undergone drastic fluctuations which, our historian will conclude, might have been expected to detach from it all but its most tenacious adherents. How, for instance, he will wonder, was it possible for those who participated in the adulations of the early heroes of the Revolution so readily to accept their downfall, and to believe them to have been guilty from the beginning of ideological heresy and acts of treachery of the most heinous kind? In that remarkable period between September, 1939, and June, 1941, when Ribbentrop received the Order of Lenin, and Molotov was an honoured guest in Berlin, and Stalin and Hitler exchanged cordial and congratulatory messages, did doubts arise in the Canterbury Deanery? Did that forward looking couple, the Webbs, begin to wonder if, after all, the Fabian rainbow ended at the Kremlin?

Not at all. The Webbs were silent, and the Dean had 'the highest authority for stating that there had been no conversations between Russia and Germany before August, 1939', and that the conversations, when they took place, 'contained no plan for partitioning Poland between Germany and the Soviet Union'. Bombs dropped on Helsinki did not apparently shake the faith of the pacifist Friends of the Soviet Union that the cause of peace was safe in Stalin's hands, any more than a vast sharing out of spoils with Nazi Germany appeared to diminish the conviction that the only faithful adherents of the anti-Fascist cause were the rulers of Russia.

Our historian is likely, indeed, to be unable to withhold a certain admiration from a faith so touchingly persistent. Cherished revolutionary leaders might be trampled in the dust and disclosed as enemies of the Soviet Fatherland; the Party Line might change with startling suddenness, holding up to obloquy what had been venerated and vice-versa; but in Senior Common Rooms, in the columns of progressive weeklies, in remote Passfield Corner and in the venerable Canterbury Deanery, the stock of the Russians continues to rise. Inconsistency could not tarnish their reputation. Neither immoderate demands for reparations nor the irresponsible exercise of the veto at Lake Success could wean from them the allegiance of those accustomed to be foremost in insisting that reparations were an imperialistic device and the undue influence of the Great Powers an abomination.

Finding in this line of inquiry no solution to his dilemma, out historian might well turn from the general to the particular. If fellow-travelling made no sense in terms of policy, it might be comprehensible in terms of individual psychology. What, he might ask himself, was it in the character of fellow-travellers which made them persist in a point of view alien to their own professed principles and inimical to their own interests? Why, when they were confronted with the spectacle of the liquidation of their like elsewhere, did they persist in inviting the same fate? If the concentration camps in Eastern Germany and other areas under Russian occupation or influence were full of social democrats and pacifists and intellectuals, did it not occur to them that the coming to pass of what they so ardently advocated would make them also inmates?

Did the execution of a Liberal like Petkov, the flight of a Socialist like Mikolajczyk, have no moral for them? Meditating upon this, our historian might recall an apposite thought of Taine's relating to sympathisers with the French Revolution, some of whom, interestingly enough, remained faithful even after Napoleon had taken over. Nothing is more dangerous, the French historian wrote, than a general idea in a narrow mind. It ferments there like yeast, coming in time to dominate all the mental activity of the individual concerned until, in the most literal sense, he is 'possessed'.

The fellow-traveller today is in a like case. He has ceased to be able to relate his obsession either to his own interests, or to any coherent system of thought. Reason and self-preservation, those two essential ingredients in a civilised existence, have ceased to be applicable. He is, as Taine puts it, 'possessed'. Argument does not impinge upon him, and the normal restraints of prudence are not operative. He is ready, even eager, to eat yesterday's words, and to denounce yesterday's hero. He derives no moral from the melancholy fate of others who, for instance, in Czechoslovakia, have taken the same position as he has. Not even Tito's sudden fall from favour abates his zeal. The only hope for him is exorcism, so that the Gadarene swine may hurl themselves to destruction in his place.

8

HEROES OF THEIR TIME: BERTRAND RUSSELL AND D H LAWRENCE

The celebrity which is nowadays so lavishly and instantaneously bestowed, often proves to be surprisingly transient. Where Victorian heroes loomed ever larger after decease, with long-winded, adulatory biographies as signposts along the road to posthumous fame, ours have but to turn up their toes to be largely forgotten. When there are adulatory biographies, more often than not they provide an occasion rather for marvelling at a personality cult that is past than for reviving its practice.

Witness Ronald W Clark's massive tribute to the late Bertrand Russell. I suppose mathematical specialists still have occasion to make honourable mention of his *Principia Mathematical* (written in collaboration with AN Whitehead), and students majoring in philosophy to turn over the pages of his *History of Western Philosophy*. No doubt pious nuclear disarmers are liable to look back nostalgically on the great days of the Aldermaston marches, and there may even be aspiring free-lovers, progressive educationalists and anti-God zealots who refresh themselves from time to time by returning to Russell's writings on such themes. Of course, too, his name crops up frequently in memoirs and other documentation, especially relating to the Bloomsbury set, now decidedly in fashion. Here, his frequent stays at Garsington Manor, and intimate relationship with Lady Ottoline Morrell, the presiding goddess, ensures him honourable mention, along with Lytton Strachey, Aldous Huxley, DH Lawrence and other frequenters of her court.

Even so, all the way through Clark's well-researched, and well-written tribute to Russell I keep asking myself whether his subject really rated such ample and assiduous treatment. Was Russell, as Clark indomitably insists, a great thinker, a master-mind, a seer, even a rather special kind of near-saint? Or, as I have long believed myself, no more than a quick-witted, excessively randy, displaced earl, who managed to shock his way into being noticed, first academically, then as an authority on shifting contemporary *mores*, and finally, thanks to the joint efforts of the Kremlin and his Svengali-like secretary, Ralph Schoenman, as a figure of world significance in the shaping of foreign policy and the defining of international relations?

My own impressions of his polemical writings, in which I have had occasion to browse from time to time, and of his radio and television disputations when I have been a participant, is that his thinking was superficial, his intellectual bigotry fluctuating and often absurd, and his capacity for making irresponsible dogmatic statements, limitless. Indeed, in the light of the inconstancy of his views, the recklessness of his pronouncements on contemporary affairs (he once bet me 20 pounds that Sen. Joseph McCarthy would infallibly be elected President of the United States on the completion of Eisenhower's first term), and his readiness to throw out highly biased opinions on everything under the sun, from the poet Wordsworth to the Crucifixion, it must be considered extraordinary that he continued to be revered as a man of learning and sagacity.

Here, some observations by Thomas Gray, author of *Elegy written in a Country Churchyard* – lines which at one time all schoolboys were expected to learn by heart – on how Lord Shaftesbury came to have philosophical credentials, may be relevant. They are quoted in Dr Johnson's incomparable *Lives of the English Poets*:

'You say you cannot conceive how Lord Shaftesbury came to be a philosopher in vogue; I will tell you. First, he was a lord; secondly, he was as vain as any of his readers; thirdly, men are very prone to believe what they do not understand; fourthly, they will believe anything at all provided they are under obligation to believe it; fifthly, they love to take a new road even when that road leads nowhere; sixthly, he was reckoned a fine writer, and seemed always to mean more than he said. Would you have any more reasons? An interval of above forty years has pretty well destroyed the charm. A dead lord ranks with commoners: vanity is no longer interested in the matter; for a new road has become an old one.'

It seems to me to fit Russell like a glove, and will surely seem even more apposite by the year 2010 when he will have been dead 40 years.

It is greatly to Clark's credit that, while maintaining his attitude of awed reverence for Russell's gifts and attainments, as far as can be seen he makes no effort to fake the evidence. This would, in any case, have been a difficult, and even risky, undertaking in view of Russell's relentless, if not shameless, candour about himself in his autobiography; particularly regarding his non-stop amours, whether at the elevated level of his long love-affair with Lady Ottoline, and, later, with Colette (Lady Constance Malleson), or of his persistent efforts to lure female admirers, the younger the better, into his bed. Not to mention his four marriages.

The long tale of his conquests, faithfully monitored by Clark, must be considered remarkable, especially in view of his scrawny appearance; the receding chin, the squeaky voice, the simian features and other intimations of biological exhaustion. Even Lady Ottoline, who, in the light of her Garsington clientèle, cannot be credited with undue squeamishness, complained of Russell's 'lack of physical attraction, the lack of charm and gentleness and sympathy.' Fame, it has been justly remarked, is a great aphrodisiac – a saying which doubtless goes far to account for Russell's notable success with what used in pre-lib days to be called the fair sex.

In Lady Ottoline's case an additional impediment was that Russell was a sufferer from pyorrhea, which, he explains, marred their physical transports. Returning from a visit to America, he was able to assure her that he had been cured of his distressing complaint, as well as passing on to her a detailed account of his seduction of Helen Dudley, the young daughter of an eminent gynaecologist who acted as his host during a stay in Chicago. While the seduction was proceeding, he tells us, Helen's three sisters obligingly 'mounted guard to give warning if either of the parents approached.'

It was scarcely a Tristan and Isolde situation, but one which, as described in his letter, served, along with the purification of his mouth, to reactivate his sexual relations with Lady Ottoline, for the enjoyment of which they repaired every Tuesday to Burnham Beeches for the day. Poor Helen Dudley, arriving in London in the middle of this rerun of an old idyll, was given a sharp brush-off by Russell on the specious grounds that, as the 1914-18 war had just broken out, and he proposed to take a leading part in opposing it, a liaison such as he had proposed in Chicago was inadmissible. 'The shock of the war,' Russell writes of the affair in his autobiography, 'killed my passion for her, and I broke her heart.' Subsequently, he goes on, she 'fell a victim to a rare disease, which first paralysed her, and then made her insane,' and concludes, in a truly philosophical vein: 'If the war had not intervened, the plan which we formed in Chicago might have brought great happiness to us both.'

The episode confirms something Leonard Woolf told me once à propos Russell – that the trouble with him was that he was utterly heartless. He just does not seem to have had any true feelings about individual people, which may explain why, on the one hand, he continued into old age writing mawkish adolescent love-letters, and, on the other, became so ardent a propagandist for humanitarian causes. As Swift pointed out, those who are most concerned about humanity seldom care much about Tom, Dick and Harry. Thus Russell, who worked himself into a lather of frenzy even in his 80s and 90s lest the men in the Pentagon or the Kremlin should blow us and our little earth to smithereens, was liable in his most intimate personal relationships to display an almost unearthly callousness.

In this respect, he may be seen as a sort of companion-piece to DH Lawrence; as Russell out of his inhumanity forged his mighty championship of humanity, so Lawrence out of his impotence forged his mighty championship of potency. The cold-hearted earl, following in the tradition of his famous grandfather, Lord John Russell, known as Radical Jack, became a sort of People's Totem, as the impotent Nottingham miner's son became the equivalent People's Phallus.

It was in Cambridge that these two gimcrack prophets of our time were brought together. Initially, they showered one another with compliments and planned future collaboration, but their spheres of interest overlapped too much for harmonious relations to prove durable, and soon they were screaming insults. Lawrence was able to get in a fell blow with one of the characters in *Women In Love* - Sir Joshua Malleson, 'a learned, dry baronet who was always making witticisms and laughing at them heartily in a harsh horse-laugh.' Russell weighed in two decades later with a ferocious attack on Lawrence broadcast by the BBC, and may be said to have won on points.

Russell was in the habit of saying that he would most have like to live in the years before the French Revolution as a compatriot of Voltaire and the Encyclopaedists. One can quite see why - enjoying the fun of preparing a revolution but departing this world before the tumbrils called. Instead, it was his fate to live into and after the Russian Revolution. He visited the new Soviet regime in the very early days, in 1920, and reached the conclusion that it was 'a close tyrannical bureaucracy, with a spy system more elaborate and terrible than the Tsar's ... No vestige of liberty remains, in thought or speech or action. I was stifled and oppressed by the weight of the machine as by a cope of lead.'

In his book *The Practice and Theory of Bolshevism* he wrote about the regime in this strain, in splendid contrast with the sycophantic and abysmally credulous reactions of other intellectuals like Shaw, the Webbs, Gide, Barbusse, etc. etc. Yet before even Russell's words were printed, on his way to China, when his fellow-passengers asked him to speak about Russia, he felt bound to say 'only favourable things about the Soviet Government.'

It was the ultimate *Trahison des clercs*, and epitomizes what was to be the practice of the flower of our Western intelligentsia in the tumultuous years to come, whereby they have been instrumental in undermining and invalidating all the values and aspirations they purported to be upholding, in the process, incidentally, abolishing themselves. In this sense, Russell may be seen as the foremost intellectual of his time, and also the last one of genius; the voice of one crying in the wilderness to make straight the way for the outpouring of meaningless words and the repetition of mindless slogans which lay ahead.

Ferreting about in contemporary letters, as even so unsystematic and unscholarly a book critic as myself will from time to time, the figure of DH Lawrence looms up inescapably. I very much wish it were not so. How often I have closed one of the many outpourings about him with the thought that never, but never, will I so much as open another, come what may! Then another appears on the scene, perhaps by one of those unspeakable women who gathered round him, and I'm at it again, hooked!

Now at least I can hope that my addiction will henceforth be fed from a single source. By a happy chance I find myself in possession of Edward Nehsl's three-volume *D.H. Lawrence: A Composite Biography*, a magnificent piece of scholarship containing pretty well everything of significance written about Lawrence, whether by his friends and associates or by himself, all chronologically arranged, judiciously chosen, conveniently and exhaustively annotated, with an excellent index and bibliography. Next time I pine for a fix I shall turn to Mr. Nehls instead of sucking down, say, some of Frieda Lawrence's raw spirit or Middleton Murry's rancid cider, and calm will be restored.

One chapter of Mr. Nehls's vast work riveted my attention for a particular reason: 1908-1912: Croydon, when I was at an elementary school in Croydon, Lawrence was teaching at another, and my teacher, Helen Corke, was a close friend of his, spending much of her spare time with him. Thus I was able, in considering this phase of Lawrence's life, to fill in the background in a quite personal and vivid way. Also, I recently had a long televised conversation with Miss Corke - now an old lady in her eighties, but not all that older than me in my middle sixties - about her relations with Lawrence and her memories of him as a fellow teacher in Croydon.

Those early elementary or board schools were built on a standard plan provided by the old Board of Education. They had an air more of prisons than of schools, standing up stark and gaunt, all with a regulation asphalt playground into which the children were turned for their morning and afternoon break. I've never seen anything quite like them in America; they belonged, I fancy, to a phase of our Victorian social history which never got across the Atlantic. In the public estimation they were for the poor and the lowly; we who went to them, especially in a predominantly middle- or lower-middle-class South London suburban area like Croydon, were considered 'rough,' and if not actual delinquents, quite close to being so. The more respectable and affluent families sent their children to fee-paying private schools where they had caps and blazers; we were educated at the public expense – in those far-off days more a stigma then, as now, a right.

The school Lawrence taught at was built at a later time than mine, and so was less dismally institutional. But it was run in the same sort of way, with an inflexible syllabus, and subject to occasional inspection by a Scotsman named Robertson, now long since dead, whom I remember well. He had masses of white hair brushed back picturesquely from a rather florid countenance, and even then I sensed something bogus in him – confirmed now by his mannered, almost patronizing account of Lawrence, included by Mr. Nehls in his composite biography. Robertson obviously didn't care much for Lawrence, and describes with some acerbity how he took him to a local literary society 'at which each member or visitor was expected to speak for some minutes on a modern poet.' (They suffered even then, didn't they? Even before the coming of TS Eliot and The Beatles.) Lawrence, it seems, chose Rachel Annand Taylor, who, he announced dramatically, according

85

to Mr. Robertson's account, had 'red hair, squirrel-red hair.' I confess I had never heard of her. This Robertson examined me once for a scholarship examination, and passed me. It was said at the time that he did it only to ingratiate himself with my father, who was on the local Education Committee. I hope it may not be so, but honesty compels me to admit that it was the only examination of the kind I ever passed.

A vivid impression abides with me of Miss Corke standing by her blackboard, or coming among us, her charges, seated at our desks, to look over our shoulders to see how we were getting on with our writing and adding. (Remember, this was fifty-eight years ago, and we were still using slates which made an excruciating scratching noise as we made marks on them.) Now I have to add to this memory the thought that not so very far away, with a similar blackboard and similar desks, DH Lawrence was standing in front of his rather older pupils. Robertson remembers him as having 'a pale face, stooping shoulders, a narrow chest, febrile hands, and a voice which I can only describe as contralto.' He and Miss Corke met most weekends, going for long walks over the Downs, talking very seriously about literature and their emotions, breaking into fragments of foreign languages - German, French - going to concerts, all part of a general cultural assiduity which belonged to people of their sort in those times.

In the light of Lady Chatterley and other Laurentian ravings about sex, it seems somehow *funny* to me now - the two of them blamelessly reading Greek plays in translation to one another, and then poor Miss Corke between whiles having to cope with my and the other children in her class's stubborn illiteracy. As I remember her in her early twenties, she was pretty and rather slight, with a lot of billowy hair; very much in the style of the mezzotint illustrations in a volume of Maupassant's short stories on my father's shelves whose pages I turned over at a very early age.

Talking it all over with Miss Corke nearly six decades later in my garden, with the arc lamps correcting the sunshine, the cameras turning, and clapper boards interrupting our talk, was a bizarre experience. To her he was 'David'; the years rolled back, and I was in her classroom learning to spell (not that I ever did); she and Lawrence facing the wind as they made their way along the coast road from Brighton via Rottingdean to Newhaven. They stayed in a boarding-house, Miss Corke recalls, at opposite ends of a long corridor, and in the middle of the night she 'woke into an intensely silent sea fog, which swathed the house like a huge, clammy spider web, and filled me with cold terror.' Terrified, she made her way along the corridor and stood outside Lawrence's room. Then she heard him talking to himself in his sleep, was reassured thereby, and returned to her bed. She described the experience in some verses she wrote, entitled *Fantasy*; Lawrence took them over, and rewrote them as *Coldness in Love*, in which it is he who stands in the corridor outside her door. Both poems exist, and shed much light, particularly on Lawrence, but also on Miss Corke and the relationship between them – so much more actual and human than Mellors' goings-on with Lady Chatterley in the woods.

Then again, Miss Corke was involved, as she told me, in a tragic happening during the time of her friendship with Lawrence. She had been having some kind of love affair, in the context of those days, with a musician who was married, with several children. After much hesitation they went away together to the Isle of Wight for a week, and then, when the musician came back and rejoined his family, in a mood of desperation he hanged himself in the bathroom. Lawrence took this tragic theme and used it for his novel *The Trespasser*, in which he calls the hero Siegmund and the heroine Helena. Together, he and Miss Corke worked over the theme, until Lawrence came to identify himself with Siegmund. Miss Corke wrote an account of the tragedy in her novel *Neutral Ground*. Some student, more diligent and scholarly than I, should find in this a fascinating subject for a thesis. Rarely can the actual process of literary composition have been so fully documented. There is also, as bearing on the same subject, Miss Corke's perceptive and well-written *D.H. Lawrence, the Croydon Years*, and now, I have heard, all the tapes of our long conversation in my garden have been deposited with the University of Texas.

Another figure in Lawrence's life who emerged into full dimensions as Miss Corke talked about her was Jessie Chambers, Lawrence's first and probably best love, the original of Miriam in *Sons and Lovers*, his good genius who helped him with his early efforts at writing, and sent off a batch of his poems to Ford Maddox Ford at the *English Review*, where they were accepted and published – his very first publication. Jessie Chambers visited Lawrence in Croydon, and she and Miss Corke became firm friends. Lawrence's behaviour over the publication of *Sons and Lovers*, which Jessie Chambers considered scurvy, led to their estrangement, and was a blow from which she never recovered. No one in my opinion understood Lawrence so well; her *D.H. Lawrence: A Personal*

Record, published under the pseudonym 'E.T.,' is a touchingly truthful account of him by someone who loved and understood him all too well.

And what of this, in a letter to Miss Corke after Lawrence's death? 'As an artist, when he is dealing with the immediate and the concrete, he is superb, but when he assays to be a thinker I find him superficial and unconvincing, and quite soon boring . . . His concern was to find some means of escape from the narrow prison of his own ego, and to do that he was prepared to assault the cosmos. So, whenever I read his almost delirious denunciations of what he pretended to regard as Christianity, I only see the caged panther lashing himself into a fury to find some way out of his strait prison. DHL was a man in bondage, and all his theorising and philosophising only bear witness to his agony.'

A man in bondage – exactly! When I compare these luminous thoughts and sentences with the congested disquisitions on Lawrence by, for instance, FR Leavis, I realize anew the chasm which divides real insight from academic criticism. 'I am sure,' Jessie Chambers concludes, 'that he broke through his prison before the end, and died a free spirit, though he had lived in bondage.' Let us hope she was right.

9

+——+

DAYSPRING FROM ON HIGH

Ever since I can remember I have [on occasion] felt myself abstracted from the world of time; impelled, in Lear's words, to take upon myself the mystery of things. As a child I had vivid recollections of this happening – walking along the road, seated in a room talking to people, and then, suddenly, almost with a click, I was not there any more; not a participant, just a spectator, looking on from afar. When I first read the phrase: 'A stranger in a strange land,' it was, to me, greatly poignant because it exactly fitted such a state of mind. Since then I've often used it in talk and writing. Sometimes there are long intervals when this feeling of being a stranger in a strange land doesn't come, so that I almost forget what it is like; but, sooner or later, it always comes back – bringing inexpressible delight.

I believe this sensation to be the basis of all religion and all art. It may be called the 'soul' in contradistinction to the body, or the imagination in contradistinction to the will. Once it has been fully experienced, all other experiences seem trivial by comparison. No perceptive human being has ever been wholly content with mortality. Man cannot live by bread alone. Looking back, it seems to me that all the happiness I have ever known has been derived from glimpses beyond mortality; from pausing, say, in the Strand, and seeing people, traffic, shops, like particles of dust caught up in sunshine and therefore momentarily existing separately. Of course, other things conduce to this state of mind, as talk, especially with a wholly sympathetic friend, and sometimes sensuality - the body then dissolving in fire rather than light, made molten rather than translucent. Beware, however, of falling into the error of a Tolstoy or a DH Lawrence, and regarding sensuality as, in itself, good or bad. Hunger is neither good nor bad, but its satisfaction deserves a grace.

My instinct has increasingly been to be abstemious, and to see in death a promise of deliverance - like one confined in a cell seeing remote blue sky through prison bars. At the same time, I have often not been abstemious, and often despaired. Peace cannot be achieved through satiety, but only through seeing beyond appetite; the idea that desire can be eliminated, by being fed is an illusion, since desire grows by what it feeds on. Not renunciation and not indulgence (the same thing really), but serenity - a harmony between flesh and spirit, between time and eternity, between living and dying. This is the peace of God which passeth all understanding; this is a state of grace.

The opposite is despair. Then time closes in on one like low-hanging clouds. Not a gleam of light breaks through anywhere. There is no horizon, and the sullen air is dry and heavy in the mouth. Then one is trapped and imprisoned indeed - a heavy iron gate which has clanged to; a windowless cell, utter silence and utter loneliness. Who, in such circumstances, would not cry out to die? Death seems the only release when there is no hope of otherwise escaping from the cold, dark dungeon of mortality. Thus situated, I have longed to die, and even tried to die.

It is the nature of the soul to soar beyond the flesh and beyond time. There are no conceivable circumstances, individual or collective, which can pin it down irretrievably to earth. Escape is always possible. I know this to be true with all my heart. The compulsions towards the earth – fear and desire and appetite– belong to the body, but ecstasy belongs to the spirit. Transmutation of the earth's compulsions into the spirit's ecstasy is being born again. In her sentimentally pious *Journal*, Eugenie de Guerin asks: 'What do you do when you are sad, you who pray no longer? What do you do when your heart is breaking?' Something in the nature of prayer – a reference of earthly unease to a comforter beyond the earth – is necessary to save hearts, and sanity, from cracking. The circumstances of mortality – irretrievably imperfect beings capable of conceiving perfection – are otherwise unendurable.

Sleeplessness, from which I suffer habitually, is an eruption of the unconscious. The mind turns round and round, like the wheels of a motor car when they will not grip; horrors invade one – shapes and ideas which embody the terrors of living; Coleridge's slimy things crawling about a slimy sea. Kipling described the condition as the night getting into his head. Thus, I dreamt of a sort of play. There was a man who was sick, and everyone was kind and considerate to him. Then in the second act he had gone mad. The curtain rose on a nurse and others playing cards on the floor, laughing; and he came on to the stage, immensely aged, bald and shrivelled, with an open book in his hand and babbling confusedly. The others paid no attention to him. On another occasion, I thought I was imprisoned and made for the window to escape, putting my hand through it, and, in the process, cutting an artery so that blood spouted up.

These are the horrors of life, the Evil One, who can be kept at bay by day, but at night can work his will. To keep him off, I try to think of all the most exquisite things I know – as, a summer's day walking through a cornfield, a warm moonlit night by the sea, a congregation in a country church at Evensong with the light of the setting sun touching the brass eagle on which the Bible stands, and say over lines I particularly like – as Donne's 'My dearest love I do not go . . .' or the collect: 'Dearly beloved brethren, I pray and beseech you as many as are here present to accompany me . . .' or the Lord's Prayer.

What is fear, which eats away at one's heart and prevents sleep? Though it attaches itself to specific things, as bodily illness or other material disasters, these only focus what exists already. They give a name to what is nameless. Fear is darkness; fear is being excluded from the society of God; fear is servitude to fleshly appetites. The only way to exorcise fear is by its opposite, love – perfect love which casteth out fear. The more love there is in a human heart, the less room there is for fear. Without love a vacuum is set up which fear soon rushes in to fill. The same thing is true of a society. When it is based on the concept of hatred, its only mystique is fear. Everyone has to be afraid in order to hate; everyone has to hate in order to go on being afraid.

In Russia, in Hitler's Germany, one sensed the omnipresence of fear – the sudden knock at the door, and everyone growing pale; the fear in people's eyes, the furtive looks. When I left Russia by train, just across the Letvian frontier where there was a white stake in the ground with a G.P.U. man in his familiar long grey overcoat standing beside it, one of the passengers went out into the corridor and shook his fist in the direction whence we had come. We all spontaneously joined him and did likewise; then began to laugh hysterically. We had been delivered from the kingdom of fear.

Since that time its bounds have been greatly extended. Even, however, if they encompassed the whole world, it would not be for ever. Men look towards the light and away from the darkness; their hearts yearn after love, and release from fear. As a prisoner, however deep his dungeon, and however long he has been incarcerated there, never quite forgets the delights of liberty, so in the sunless land of fear there can never be any enduring acclimatisation. Though whole generations pass away, still in the soul of man there is the longing to behold the radiance of God's love whence he is derived. Flowers in dark places which never feel the sun still lift their blooms in its direction, for such is their nature.

Efforts to establish a Kingdom of Heaven on Earth are wholly misguided, and those, like Gandhi and Tolstoy, who undertake the attempt are led inevitably into falsity. Thus, Tolstoy suffering the humiliation of having armed guards on his estate to prevent the peasants from stealing timber, and Gandhi being involved in Swaraj politics. The point is that perfection cannot be instituted in terms of imperfection, but imperfection can strive after perfection in terms of itself. It is the difference between the steeple of Salisbury Cathedral reaching into the sky and the Tower of Babel intended to mount to Heaven. The one is exquisite in its aspiration, the other ludicrous in its pretension; the one serene, the other clamorous and discordant. Tolstoy wanted to be wholly good and wholly spiritual; but in abolishing his appetites by the will he only enraged them, putting himself in the pitiable situation of fornicating furiously and disgustedly when he was seventy and over, abandoning home and wife when he was eighty. Appetite cannot be willed out of existence, but only, by God's grace, transubstantiated – dying in the flesh and being re-born in the spirit.

+⊱━⊰+

Walking through the streets of London, individual restlessness comprehended in a collective restlessness – traffic, passers by, all caught up in the same essential rhythm, like dead leaves caught up in the autumnal wind. No destination or purpose, except just to move as others are moving; the bright green grass of Regent's Park, varying shops towards whose windows lingering glances, faint desires, are cast, evening papers mechanically offered and taken. Then down Baker Street, through Portman Square, on to Hyde Park Corner in the Spring sunshine, houses in Park Lane newly painted, green shutters bright as the green grass. At Hyde Park Corner itself the orators declaiming, words cast into the air and falling they know not where; faces distorted as with passion, angrily persuasive, clamorous and insistent – venerable figure, little heeded, sternly beseeching: 'Prepare to meet thy God!', placard to this effect displayed; heavily bearded exponent of some ancient lost cause, and another with studied oratory, a crucifix beside him, recommending the Catholic faith.

Vast conglomeration of people, in groups, pairs or solitary – what has drawn us together, up and down, to and fro, lingering or hurrying? 'Marks of weakness, marks of woe', in each passing face; desire on the benches or under the trees; arm threaded through arm or hand contained in hand – together yet strangers, world so familiar and yet so strange, so friendly and so hostile, so dear and so terrible. These my brothers and sisters in mortality, each one entering so strangely into the kingdom of time, so strangely departing thence; comforting himself as best he may, languid or purposeful, eager or passive. I suddenly thought with great thankfulness: 'I have no grievances against anyone, no sense of having been wronged by anyone, no scores to work off or anything whatsoever to avenge. Human beings only wrong one another in so far as the person wronged agrees to be wronged. The wrong is in the recipient not the doer. I wish no ill to any living soul; if anyone were delivered into my hands for judgement I should have at once to acquit him.

A spring morning in the country – sunshine, birds singing, the grass dewy, the air fragrant, all the earth born again with the same ecstasy year by year, undaunted by the inevitability of the coming of autumn and then winter; eager only to reach the summer, that prospect sufficing. This is the pattern of the will in operation, of all earthly desires. Useless to reason – How can it go on with a ruinous end so certain? By the same token – How can spring ceaselessly repeat an exuberance which only exhausts itself in cold and desolation? Yet onto this mystery of spring, the earth's rebirth, has been grafted (or rather harmonised with it) another of vastly deeper significance – the spring or rebirth of the soul. Thus time's rhythms portray those of eternity as a smile portrays amusement. From the one the other may be deduced. One is an image of the other. If there had been no spring it would not have been possible to understand the soul's ecstasy.

A religious procession making its way along Hatton Gardens on an April Sunday seen from the top of a bus – before them a crucifix held up, and as they moved along, chanting some hymn or other. For a moment it was deeply moving, to the point of evoking tears – human souls in the deserted and ruined City, so varied in their habiliments – old and young, decrepit and vigorous, some hobbling, some striding, right at the end an aged grey lady in a bath chair, but all pressing forward after the Cross, singing as they went. This is the vision, I thought, of the saved entering the gates of the Celestial City, all singing, all confident, hobbling, shuffling, running towards the light.

Walking over Hampstead Heath, Hesketh Pearson quoted Gloucester's remark in 'King Lear' when, after he had been blinded, he said to the Old Man: 'I stumbled when I saw.' I marvelled that so brief a phrase could be so greatly moving. The whole mystery of expression in words came upon me – that a mere five should overwhelmingly convey a vast tragedy in all its implications. At the prospect of the death of someone dear thoughts on an afterlife are called in question. That face, so familiar, is to be drained of life; that voice, so often heard with delight, is never to speak again; that laughter will boom forth no more through evenings of dear companionship. These are facts before which no mere hypothesis, no mental affectation can stand up. The deep tenderness of one earth dweller for another imposes the need for an authentic solace or none at all. No platitudes or theoretical hopes will serve. Insistence in argument – To me, as to Blake, the death of the body is no more than going from one room into another – confronted with the reality of death makes a poor showing.

'Do not go,' one wants to say – as I so often have said to Hugh Kingsmill late at night trying to detain him a little longer, on seeing him home – one more turn up and down to defer parting. 'Stay a little longer.' That is the feeling now – let immortality, however sublime, be postponed in favour of some continuance of mortality, however inadequate. As a lover will barter for a caress – just one, even contemptuously bestowed – all the pretensions of a spiritual love with its pride and integrity, enduring any abasement, taking the caress as assassins take their fee. It is like seeing someone off on a train, and the train begins to move, and you run foolishly along the platform, keeping pace with the train, faster and faster, until the platform ends.

+≡≡+

Church services are very empty, and yet at their worst they have a kind of sweetness. Faces humbly downcast are more tolerable than when they are clamorous. The most terrible sight of a human being is when he is orating, face inflamed, swollen, with words; mouth gaping open like a vast, vile chasm, hands clenched. Demagogues, as Lenin and Hitler, are usually presented in this hateful posture. Even mock humility is preferable – a congregation chanting: 'We have erred and strayed in thy ways like lost sheep . .'The church service is designed to still rather than inflame the will; at least to settle the dust of living for a little while. Boys' voices convey innocence; the candles shine like truth, and the wonderful phrases of the psalms and hymns and prayers and scripture tranquillize. 'The dayspring from on High hath visited us' – I kept saying it over and over in my mind, finding it infinitely satisfying. I used to consider that the trouble about church services was that one didn't believe, so that the words of the Creed died on one's lips or were hypocritically spoken. Now, I feel differently, since I have seen that faith is more than merely believing as wisdom is more than merely knowledge.

Quite apart from any belief, whatsoever, faith, for me, maintains the following propositions:

(1) That life is more than its phenomena, and is directed towards some end which both comprehends and transcends them.

(2) That this end is benevolent, not malevolent, so that living, in any and all conceivable circumstances, is good, not bad.

(3) That the noblest pursuit of life is to attune oneself to this end, to keep one's gaze on it as a sailor does across the empty expanse of ocean for the first sight of land.

(4) That this can be done through the imagination, in contradistinction to the will; through love, in contradistinction to self-assertion; through, in the words of the New Testament, dying in the flesh to be reborn in the spirit.

(5) That desire is not the enemy of love; but its imperfect expression, as earth is the imperfect expression of heaven, and time of eternity.

(6) That the Christian religion, with all its dross, is the best expression of this everlasting truth so far available to Man, and that the civilisation based upon Christianity is the highest mode of life which has so far existed on this earth.

━━━

From the point of view of eugenics, a parent should care most for those of his children who are healthiest and most intelligent, and least for the weakest and most incompetent. In fact, it is often the other way round. I remember in Algiers, a woman with an idiot son on whom she expended all her energies and tenderness. This seemed to me more profound in its significance than any principle of eugenics.

It was a small white house where she lived, and when one opened the garden gate a bell tinkled, to warn her to come out and protect her son, interpose herself between him and strangers. He normally sat in the sun among flowers she had planted muttering to himself and sometimes trembling. If, to a visitor, he managed to ejaculate a word coherently she was as smiling and proud as if he had achieved some brilliant distinction. She tenderly translated his incoherence to visitors as a mother proudly interprets a child's first efforts to speak.

I sometimes hear that bell now; it evokes the blue sky, the flowers, the whole fragrance of love. Eugenically considered, the idiot is a useless mouth and the mother engaged in a futile pursuit; but then if the idiot had been destroyed I should have been deprived of the bell, which I can say in all sincerity is more precious to me than all the literature of eugenics with the Fabian Society thrown in. Again, biologically considered, when a woman is old and withered and barren she should legitimately be cast aside; and yet these marks of age, that withered frame, are the very pattern of love, as a sunset is the glory of a summer's day, or as the exquisite colours of autumn recall in tranquillity the ecstasy of spring.

+≻══≺+

The will is insatiable in all its appetites, haunted by fear, spurred on by desire which grows by what it feeds on, its only conceivable outcome the Gadarene swine blindly, inevitably hurling themselves to destruction. There is no release from the will through the will. Release is possible only by the destruction of the will followed by re-birth in the spirit. Whatever might happen to the world, to the Christian Church, to me and mine, this will always be true; in the realisation of its truth may I be delivered from fear. The destruction of the will cannot be willed, but is achievable only through God's grace. Every indulgence in desire feeds and strengthens the will – as alcohol, fornication in thought and deed. How I long sometimes to be delivered from desire, envying the dead because their appetites have died with their flesh; saying over to myself those last words of Cromwell – 'It is not my desire to eat or to sleep, but to make what haste I may to begone.'

Yet the wonder of life is that it is possible to die in the flesh and be reborn in the spirit without waiting for death. There is escape from the prison before the sentence is served. How I wish I could keep this always before me, reading what embodies it, eschewing anger and lust and hatred, all the will's brood, fixing my eyes beyond the horizon of time and my spirit beyond the confines of flesh. There is no doubt now, and never has been any doubt, that therein lies all joy, all blessedness, all true achievement. Everything else is vanity, and at last anguish and madness. There is nothing worth thinking about except eternity, and nothing worth feeling except love, which is the soul's delight. Beyond the tallest spire, beyond the furthest view, beyond all thought and aspiration and excellence - [there] I would be, and abide ever.

There is no imagery adequate to the purpose. Mortal love is sweet, but compared with this other, only bitter. When it reigns, material things are shadows, and men and women tread the streets silently, as though pavements were covered with deep snow. 'Be not afeard, be not afeard,' I say to myself. Fear has no meaning when perfect love casts it out. What should I fear for? - this mortal life of mine? It soon must end in any case. This mortal society to which I belong? It, too, infallibly, will perish tomorrow or the day after, and, like enough, as others have, leave little or nothing behind to show that it ever was. These small possessions, these dear ones, this corner of my own? They, likewise, are mortal, and cannot be defended against the ravages of time, which washes over them, and all else, like huge breakers on a sandy coast. I have no stake in the world, or would not have any, and cannot lose what I do not have. I would arrive in eternity like a happy traveller, unencumbered with baggage, or regrets, or letters-of-credit. When the world has truly no power to hold me, then am I free indeed; then only truly delivered from all evil.

It is easy for weeks on end to be wholly submerged in the world of time - like a watchmender who, with magnifying glass screwed in his eye, sees nothing but the minute machinery he is repairing. How strange this will seem looked back on across eternity - my soul among the billions and billions which have existed, now exist, and will exist hereafter, with a vast desert of time stretching into the past and another reaching into the future, living for a few decades on a speck of dust riding through the universe; mysteriously born, and then, shortly after, as mysteriously dying; and yet, absorbed in these circumstances, as a moth is in the brightness round which it flutters; as a worm is in the dark earth through which it burrows. How terrible for man is this absorption! How miserable, wretched and lost when the waves of time close over one's head, and its salt is in one's mouth. To look beyond mortality! To see the glimmer of light where the dawn will break, and to hear sweet sounds in the distance growing imperceptibly nearer!

How am I to lose the world, break the bonds of time, breathe not the stale air of mortality but the fresh breezes of eternity, live in terms of everlasting reality instead of the delusions of sense, keep my gaze fixed on God, from whom alone comes peace. Like as the hart panteth after the water brook, tongue parched, eyes wild with longing, so do I yearn for eternity, and cannot find satisfaction in anything else; not in eating or drinking or in the indulgence of any appetite; not in the wonders of the world or human companionship or love or lust, in life or in death, in work or in idleness, in contemplation or in restless movement, in riches or in poverty, in fame or in obscurity, in understanding or in folly. No other food will do, no other joy will substitute.

'And there were the dishes in which they brought to me, being hungry, the Sun and Moon instead of Thee,' St. Augustine cried regarding his secular studies. I, too, have a hunger which the Sun and Moon will not satisfy. Its satisfaction is the only pursuit I care for; that it exists, provides the certainty that the wherewithal to satisfy it also exists – as the fact of physical hunger presupposes the existence of bread. There is no name for this hunger except love, and only in the self's obliteration can it be satisfied. It has existed since the beginning of time, and will exist till the end of time. For me, a Western European. I find its most perfect formulation in the New Testament, and, especially, in the First Epistle of St. John.

How extraordinary is this longing, every day more intense – for what? I scarcely know – for perfection, for eternity, for that peace which the world cannot give; a longing to begone, and yet not a desire for death such as one feels in moments of despair; a consciousness of having some part in a purpose transcending time and space, of hearing distant music, of being in love, but not with another human being – rather with life itself, and death, and all creation; pain, disappointment and other ills only like blemishes on a loved face which make it the more lovable. I often say over Caliban's words – 'This Isle is full of noises, sounds and sweet airs . . .', and think of his dreams, so wonderful that when he waked he cried to sleep again. Yet the ecstasy cannot be conveyed.

A watery, wintry dawn seen across London roofs is exceed-ingly lovely. It is as though the old Thames were once more flowing through deserted, desolate marshes. In the stillness, London seems only a dream, a shadow, with no corporeal existence. Seeing it thus, I reflected that the greatness of Christian civilization, of which London is a manifestation, derives from the religion out of which it was born. Through-out all its cruel history, the idea has been kept alive that men belong to one family, with one father in Heaven, and so must be brothers one with another. However imperfectly, this concept finds expression in law, in art, in all institutions, in the whole apparatus of society. Materialism, whether in the American or the Russian version, is the exact antithesis of such a concept. It claims for the ego all rights because there is nothing but the ego, and therefore leads back to barbarism, to the condition before civilization existed. This is absolutely and irretrievably the consequence of setting up Man as his own God. Thither we are now moving, with what accompa-niment of horrors cannot be imagined. I feel this deluge upon me, and ask only that I may be vouchsafed the strength to live out what remains of my own days, in the light of truth as I have seen it - that Man lives in so far as the ego dies, that self-abnegation is greater than self-assertion, that to bow the head before the wonder and mystery of creation is more fitting than to raise it in defiance, and that the imagination alone can light a path through the forests of the night - Paul, Blake, Beethoven, Constable and many, many others contributing to that sublime radiance.

Goodness has an aroma of sweetness, evil a stench. This is not fanciful, but a fact. Between the powers of darkness operating through the will, and those of light operating through the imagination or soul, there is ceaseless war – a conflict which takes place collectively, as well as inside each individual. This recalls an image in 'The Pilgrim's Progress' – Christian, climbing up a mountain in the shade keeps seeing round each bend the sunshine in which he longs to be but never reaches. Like all Bunyan's images, it is perfect because it recalls an exact experience. How excluded one feels in the chill shade when one sees the earth bathed in sunshine, seemingly near, yet out of reach. So it is possible to be excluded from goodness. 'Lighten our darkness, we beseech thee,' is, perhaps, the most poignant of all prayers. It is also true that goodness exists by virtue of itself and not by virtue of the acts it induces. Goodness in itself spreads light; the halo is an authentic phenomenon. The mere presence of goodness destroys its opposite as light destroys darkness. Nothing needs to be said, or even done. In the presence of goodness anger is consumed, arrogance expires, lustfulness flickers out – a fire without fuel.

For days, and even weeks, the light can be lost sight of, the task forgotten. Then, in a despairing moment, remembrance comes, and resolution is again summoned up. There is no other answer to despair – neither drug nor stimulant, neither sleep nor wakefulness; no change of scene, or of companionship, or of way of life; no satiety of the senses. This is a hunger which bread will not satisfy, a thirst which drink will not quench. The only satisfaction lies in self-abnegation; the way, as the New Testament says, is narrow, and the gate to it is straight. Yet along this way alone is life worth living; can, indeed, be lived at all. Generalised plans for human felicity are all doomed, not merely to failure, but to produce the exact opposite of what was intended. Each individual must find the way alone and follow it alone. Who knows what future horrors the pursuit of collective chimera may hold. It may even be that Man, in the Will's final frenzy, will blow the earth itself to pieces, and himself with it. No matter. All that will be lost is a speck of dust travelling through the universe - that's nothing. What remains is eternity and Man's part in it - that's everything.

10

TWO WRITERS: SOMERSET MAUGHAM AND LEONARD WOOLF

A visit to Somerset Maugham at the Villa Mauresque was always memorable and enjoyable, though latterly, of course, in view of his condition, liable to be painful. His folded, parchment face and small glittering eyes; his elegant, but somehow not quite 'correct' attire, clothing a body which was neat, slight and wiry; yet likewise, in some indefinable way, distorted and infirm; the stutter which varied between making speech almost impossible and being barely noticeable, according to his mood and the company he kept; the villa itself, with its large, carefully tended garden, swimming-pool and other appurtenances of affluence, the well-run household, the luncheon excellent, simple and invariable, always the same inscrutable servants opening the door and waiting at table; with this ostensible luxury, a decided flavour of parsimony, of a careful, even somewhat grudging, hand in control – it all added up to a single impression. Of what? I remember asking myself the first time I went there. The answer was obvious when one came to think about it. Maugham lived in the style and spirit of one of his own short stories.

The touch of 'commonness,' the skill and ingenuity, the sentimentality masquerading as cynicism, the false values so appetisingly served up from China to Peru; wherever two or more were gathered together in clubs, messes, P & O liners, *wagons-lit*, with the dawn coming up like thunder, out of Sevenoaks, 'crost the Thames – were not these precisely the characteristics of life in the Villa Mauresque, shining in the Riviera sun where Cap Ferrat juts into the blue Mediterranean? Romantic writers are forced to dwell in their own illusions, to build them into little houses which, like snails, they carry on their backs, retreating into them when danger – that's reality – threatens. Thus, poor old Snow shuffling along the corridors of power, Waugh for ever revisiting Brideshead, Hemingway living dangerously to the point, in the end, of blowing out his own brains; thus Maugham on the Côte d'Azur, where the brown bodies with their delicate bikini tracings are packed side by side, stretching from Cap Ferrat to eternity. Truly, God is not mocked.

The thing I like best about Maugham, and found most admirable, was his total lack of literary pretentiousness. He just never thought of himself, or behaved, as a great writer. If anything, he underrated his own work, seeing himself as a popular entertainer merely, who would soon be forgotten. Actually, 'Cakes and Ale' (his own favourite, as he told me once) is, in my opinion, a much better novel than many which are more highly regarded today. His comments on other writers were shrewd and perceptive, and never governed by current fads and fashions. His attitude towards contemporary mandarins like T.S. Eliot was well this side of idolatry. The craftsman in him – far and away his predominant side as a writer – steadied him in making literary judgments. It was a great pleasure, and most beneficial, to listen to him when he talked about the technicalities and practice of writing.

For critics generally he professed contempt, and, unlike other successful writers, never seemed to bother much about reviews. Perhaps he resented a little the lack of esteem for his work among highbrows. I know he sometimes let fall a sigh in the direction of Rapallo along the coast, where Max Beerbohm was growing ever more famous in literary and intellectual circles with every book he did not write. Someone once remarked at his table that a small fund was being raised, sponsored by Eliot, to provide Beerbohm with a wireless set. Maugham's irritation at this ludicrous project was evident. His stutter became convulsive. Why, he seemed to be asking, reward indolence when his own steady industry brought him so little esteem? Such mighty sails for so tiny a craft!

In general, however, he was well content with his lot. He liked being rich and took pleasure in the thought that his earnings from his pen had probably set a record. Forgive me, AP Herbert, but there has never been a time when successful writers could so enrich themselves. Even in a league which included Shaw, Wells, Wodehouse, Kipling, Galsworthy, etc., Maugham's earnings have been prodigious. His satisfaction at being wealthy has been more due to vanity than to self-importance or self-indulgence. His ways were relatively simple and abstemious. Like all timid, lonely people, money seemed to him a protection. It set up a buffer between him and a largely alien and hostile world. To this end he sought it, first diligently and ardently, and finally as an addiction.

Contrary to popular view, far from being 'cynical,' Maugham's temperament was romantic, if not sentimental. I remember that on one occasion he described with great feeling how at some public function he had seen the Windsors and they were holding hands. Was it not a touching proof, he said, that their romance, which cost him so dear in worldly terms, had proved worthwhile? The impression of Maugham which nothing will efface is of an outsider. Of the many who have claimed that honorific title of our time, he unquestionably deserved it. He had many acquaintances among what he would call, with a deprecating smile, the great; Churchill and Beaverbrook, for instance. Visitors were frequent at the Villa Mauresque, and included a variety of notabilities. Yet Maugham was never, as it were, fully integrated into this world of the eminent and successful, even though he ostensibly upheld its credentials. Particularly latterly, he spent much of his time alone, or in the company of his faithful friend and secretary, Alan Searle, whose exacting devotion to him over many years deserves the highest commendation.

What, then, set Maugham apart? Not, certainly, any mystical leanings. He was the least religious of men. Nor did he, like Swift, come to sicken of the company of his fellows. In principle, he remained gregarious and companionable. Was it, perhaps, his early poverty? His not very happy childhood? His homosexuality? The failure of his marriage? I should not have thought so. Plenty of people with these, and worse, afflictions, and far less gifted and successful than Maugham, have managed to come to terms with their circumstances. Maugham, it seems to me, never did. It was this side of his character which appealed to me and made me feel always affectionately disposed to him; a sort of fastidiousness, an essential integrity which held him aloof. At the end of a long life full of fame and wealth and distinction, he remained triumphantly an outsider.

The last time I visited the Villa Mauresque he had just got rid of his pictures in consequence of some tiresome and unedifying family row. The spaces on the walls where they had hung still showed. He complained bitterly that he missed them, and I blurted out, for once carried away in his company, how all any of us wanted was that he should have for his remaining years whatever satisfaction life could offer, and so on. I don't think he even heard what I said; deafness increasingly afflicted him. In any case, it was no business of mine. I think of him now, and always shall when I look down on Cap Ferrat – an old, old man staring forlornly at those empty spaces on his walls, indomitable even in his wilfulness; a craftsman whose steady application and accomplished performance in the field of English letters must deserve the respect and the envy of other practitioners.

+‡=‡=‡+

I shall always think of Leonard Woolf in his lovely garden at Rodmell, in Sussex. It was part of the serenity of his temperament – he was the most serene person I have ever known – to love his garden the more for its association with his wife Virginia, even though it also recalled her tragic self-inflicted death. In one of its more enchanting corners there was a bust of her, and there I sat with him on a summer's afternoon talking about her without any sense of unease or restraint.

Woolf, as he told me, had no belief in or expectation of immortality. He was entirely convinced he would never see Virginia again, or continue to exist in any way himself when his earthly life ended. There was no despair or even drama in this for him. He was a true stoic. He lived his life nobly and austerely, and, I am sure, relinquished it gracefully. When I heard of his death last week at the age of 88, I felt no pang of regret, such as one normally does even for the old when they pass away. In his case, it would have been unbecoming. All I felt was gratitude for the time I spent in his company. Though we disagreed fundamentally, I found a sort of inspiration in him. I loved his simple way of life, his utter honesty and truthfulness, his patience and dedication to work, his innumerable acts of kindness and consideration to all sorts and conditions of people. To village people whom he delighted to help and know. To Bloomsbury survivors like Labokova with whom he invariably ate his Christmas dinner. To fellow gardeners for whom he organised an annual show.

Up to the end he largely did for himself. Luncheon invariably consisted of bread and cheese, slices of tongue, lemonade from the great jug he made himself, or beer. The passion for goodness was not in him. But the practice was. He was an extraordinarily good man. One of the many touching pictures that emerged was of him and Virginia together setting the type for printing, on their flat-bed press, the very first edition of 'The Waste Land.' This was the beginning of the Hogarth Press, which they founded and which throve, in terms of prestige and finance. Woolf told me that his original idea had been that typesetting might prove an effective therapy for Virginia's mental disturbance: I find this kindly notion more estimable than the result – the launching of a thousand seminaries on Eliot's preposterously overrated poem.

Woolf will, of course, be for ever associated with the Bloomsbury set. I always felt that, although he belonged to them, he was in many respects different. Thus he was born into an affluent and cultivated Jewish family, but after his father's early death they were in straitened circumstances – something which few of the other Bloomsburyites ever experienced. Then, as a highly efficient civil servant in Ceylon (no one, incidentally, has given a better account of what being in the old ICS was like than he in 'Growing', the first of five autobiographical volumes), he acquired a practical knowledge of government and affairs. This held him in good stead as secretary of the Labour Party's advisory committees on international and imperial affairs and as a publisher. He justly prided himself on being a capable administrator and man of business. Finally, he was too nice and too sensitive to feel the sense of superiority over other mortals with which Virginia, her sister Vanessa and her husband, Clive Bell, Lytton Strachey, and the others were afflicted.

He saw very clearly the faults of Fabians like the Webbs, and had numerous highly diverting anecdotes about them. His judgments were shrew and sound; as when he said about Bertrand Russell that he was cold and without feeling. Even his close friends, even Virginia, he weighed up justly and dispassionately. I sometimes thought that in the last resort he did not care greatly for humans at all, and much preferred animals; especially dogs, who were his constant companions. He communicated with them with uncanny skill, and came, as it seemed to me, to look like them. I am sure that at Rodmell their barking is hushed and muted now. If I were to address a letter of sympathy about his death to anyone, it would be to them.

Woolf's socialism and internationalism (he was one of the first to envisage a League of Nations in his 'International Government,' first published in 1915 as a supplement to the lately-founded *New Statesman*) were consistently and sincerely held, but against a background of an essentially pessimistic attitude to his times. He believed in his heart that all the liberal hopes plausibly entertained for our Western civilisation expired in the First World War, never to be seriously revived. Even so, he worked on, to the very last day of his life, concerned about injustice, cruelty, oppression and all other impediments to ameliorating our human condition.

11

THE PROPHET OF SEX

There are few things more repulsive than picturesque old men. If ever I find myself cultivating a venerable white beard and hair to match I shall know that the end has come. The thought is put in my mind by looking at the picture of Havelock Ellis on the dust-jacket of his autobiography, first published in 1940 and now reissued. To be vain about youthful good looks is permissible, though still not edifying; one remembers with distaste all the high-table camp talk about Rupert Brooke's good looks (for instance, Lytton Strachey's high-pitched 'Rupert in *en beauté* tonight' on catching a glimpse of him at a theatre) among Cambridge homosexuals. But to be vain amidst the foliage of old age is disgusting, and betokens an obsessive narcissism.

Ellis was a classic example. His body, he indicates in *My Life*, gave off sweet smells; 'my mother when she kissed me used often to say that my cheeks were scented, and my wife, who has frequently made the same remark, has also said that my cast-off shirts have a distinct odour of cedar.' His head, he writes, passed for being 'noble', his eyes for being bright and beautiful; 'Olive Schreiner said once of my nude form

that it was like that of Christ in the carpenter's shop in Hol-
man Hunt's *Shadow of the Cross*'. On another occasion Olive
Schreiner compared him to the 'eager, bright-eyed satyr in
Rubens's picture, *Silenus*'. A 'dear friend lived to call me
'Faun', and Edward Carpenter, with the quiet twinkle of his
luminous eyes, once said to me: 'He is the god Pan.'

Faun or Pan or Christ, or all three at once, Ellis clearly had
a great and abiding passion for himself. He works lovingly
over his limbs, features and organs, only leaving out the geni-
tals, one feels, because they were too sacred in his eyes to be
included even in this auto-erotic survey. Nothing clouded the
serenity of his relationship with himself; they never, as it were,
spoke a cross word to one another – he and himself. It was
a perfect marriage, and if there were occasional infidelities –
with his wife Edith, with Olive Schreiner, with 'Amy' who
turns out to have been the daughter of his friend Dr Baker
Smith, with Margaret Sanger, the early American contracep-
tion evangelist, and with Françoise Delisle the companion
of his last years, actually a French woman named Françoise
Lafitte-Cyon – his only true love and dear companion was
himself.

With so narcissistic a temperament Ellis was bound to find
his relations with women – to put it mildly – unusual and
delicate. Alan Hull Walton, in his introduction to this new
edition of *My Life*, insists that Ellis was neither impotent nor
homosexual. We must take his word for it, though none of the
relationships with women described in *My Life* can be considered as normal, or, in the accepted sense, sexually satisfying.
His wife turned out to be a lesbian, and after their marriage soon reverted to lesbian practices. In the end the poor

woman went off her head, becoming, except in occasional lucid moments, fiercely hostile towards Ellis. Olive Schreiner, with whom he was according to his own account in love, was clearly a passionate woman (Ellis called her 'lion' and she him 'my soul's wife'), but their indulgence in sensuality together, such as it was, can scarcely have been, from her point of view, up to scratch. Some idea of how it went is perhaps conveyed by the following bizarre incident:

'I see her at her rooms at Hastings where I had come to spend the week-end with her, bringing at her desire my student's microscope, for she wished to observe living sper-matozoa, which there was no difficulty in obtaining to place under the cover glass for her inspection, and I see her interest in their vigorous mobility.'

This is not, I should suppose, quite what Antony and Cleo-patra were up to.

What precisely happened with Amy, his mistress of sorts over a number of years, is not even hinted at, but rightly or wrongly one has the impression that with her, too, it was the by-ways rather than the main stream of sexual passion along which they ventured. Of all his lady friends Amy seems to have been the most quiescent, and may well have been called on to indulge his proneness to urolagnia (his own word) which he considers he inherited from his mother, to whose 'early love of water' he draws attention:

'Once at the age of twelve she took me to spend the day at the London Zoological Gardens. In the afternoon as we were walking side by side along a gravelled path in a solitary part of the Gardens, she stood still, and soon I heard a very audible stream falling to the ground. When she moved on I instinctively glanced behind at the pool in the path, and my mother, having evidently watched my movements, remarked shyly: 'I did not mean you to see that.' ... No doubt there was a shy alarm as to what her now tall, serious boy would think of this new experience with his mother, but there was also the impulse to heighten a pleasurable experience by blending with it the excitement of sharing it with her son.'

Later, he writes, he became interested in vesical energy, and published a paper on 'The Bladder as a Dynamometer'. 'My vision of this function,' he goes on, 'became in some degree attached to my feeling of tenderness towards women - I was surprised how often women responded to it sympathetically.' This view was confirmed when his sister Louie said of his mother's behaviour in the Zoological Gardens: 'She was flirting with you.' As for Françoise - by the time Ellis joined up with her he was getting on in years, and even his urolagnia had doubtless begun to lose its edge. Françoise, in any case, was well armed. Had she not called herself, in a fragment of autobiographical fantasy, 'The Woman Who Can Do Without A Man', all unconsciously preparing for her life with Ellis?

One naturally associates Ellis with Walt Whitman and Edward Carpenter, another picturesquely white-bearded pair in whose writings - *Leaves of Grass* and *Towards Democracy* - likewise a strong narcissistic strain is discernible. Carpenter (a largely forgotten figure now, I imagine, but in his day a name to conjure with in progressive circles) was, of course, a pioneer homosexual, and Whitman, despite repeated offers in his verses to impregnate all the daughters of America, shared the same tastes, having a fancy at one time for a street-car driver named Pete. I have read a touching account of how Whitman used to ride to and fro on Pete's street-car, hoping to enjoy a *tête-a-tête* with him on the way to the depot when there were no other passengers. Another homosexual associate of Ellis's was John Addington Symonds, with whom he started collaborating on a work on sexual inversion. Symonds died before matters had gone very far, and Ellis, in his account of the project, disparages Symonds's contribution. One gets a rather different impression from Mrs Grosskurth's lately published brilliant biography of Symonds - not that it matters much either way.

However one looks at it, Ellis was by way of being a sexual oddity, and to that extent, one might have supposed, ill-equipped to be a guide, philosopher and friend in this particular field. Yet he, along with Kraft-Ebing and other maestros, prepared the way for - in Alan Hull Walton's words - 'undoubted giants' like Freud and Kinsey, and the so-called Sexual Revolution of our time. His *Studies in the Psychology of Sex* has been, and for all I know still may be, highly regarded; I well remember as a smutty adolescent scouring its footnotes for juvenile erotica, and seeing it displayed, along with treatises in a like vein, in what used to be known as 'rubber shops'. In a sense, indeed, he emerges from the pages of *My Life* as a true prophet, embodying, as he did, the narcissism, the self-love tapering off into impotence, of the sex-obsessed times which lay ahead.

※━━☀━━※

12

EIGHT BOOKS

M ost people would tremble at the idea of being por-
trayed to the world by a former mistress. An ex-wife
might be sour, but, up to a point at any rate, is in the same
boat as her husband. After all, she married the man, and actually bore, or was presumed ready to bear, children by him. An
ex-mistress, on the other hand, has nothing to lose, and, in the
great majority of cases, the punishment of real or imagined
wrongs to gain. Estranged lovers, alas, rarely have much regard
for one another, and often an infinity of malice.

Pablo Picasso, in any case, has suffered this fate. Mlle.
Françoise Gilot lived with him for nearly a decade, bore him
two children, and has now written what I found a quite en-
thralling account of their life together (*Life with Picasso*, by
Françoise Gilot and Carlton Lake). Her American collabora-
tor is described on the dust jacket as Paris Art Correspondent
for *The Christian Science Monitor*, a truly bizarre role in life
which I find difficulty in envisaging. The verisimilitude of the
book has been challenged, I know, by critics in a far better
position than I to judge. It has been suggested that Mlle. Gilot
affects to have remembered a great deal of Picasso's direct

speech, and that the words she puts in his mouth distort, or do not represent at all, views he is known to hold. Nonetheless, greatly daring, I venture to say that Mlle. Gilot's general account of the kind of man Picasso is in old age, and of how he is liable to expound his work, strikes me as authentic.

She first met Picasso in Paris in May, 1943, when she was a young artist. The Nazi occupation was still in full swing, and the outcome of the war still in doubt. Though known to be an ardent anti-Franco Spaniard, an advocate and leading exponent of, in Nazi eyes, 'degenerate' art, and an extreme Leftist (though not then, I think, a Communist Party member), Picasso seems to have suffered no serious molestation, or even inconvenience, at the hands of the occupation authorities. He was even able to have his studio heated – a rare privilege in those days – and just went on painting his pictures, meeting his friends (some of whom, like Malraux, were living in clandestinity), and altogether leading a more or less normal existence without reference to the war and consequent upheavals. Picasso himself, apparently, had no personal inclination to throw in his lot with the maquis or otherwise participate in anti-Nazi activities.

Mlle. Gilot only gradually became aware that Picasso's interest in her extended beyond her painting. There was, after all, a disparity of some forty years. When she did realise that his intentions were amorous, and what her parents at any rate would have considered dishonourable, she responded in a curious manner; not warmly, one way or the other, but meekly. She was ready to yield, offering no serious resistance and, equally, manifesting no serious passion. This threw Picasso. One can easily see why. To the old particularly, and to an old ram like Picasso more particularly still, a conquest is only worthwhile if it is achieved with some difficulty, apparent or real. If there is no opposition to overcome, then the haunting and enervating suspicion arises that the favours to be enjoyed are available to everyone, and that they are only accorded because the trouble of withholding them is incommensurate with the trivial inconvenience of yielding. This is deeply distressing and disturbing.

Picasso hollered like any outraged moralist. What were we coming to when well-brought-up young girls were ready at the drop of a hat to fall in with the advances of an old fellow like himself? Subsequently, of course, they did become lovers. The first decisive step was when Mlle. Gilot allowed herself to be undressed by Picasso, who then stood apart, carefully and deeply studying her nude form. I find this very touching. The one great passion in Picasso's life is for visual art, to which everything else - even lechery - must take second place. Only when he had looked his fill in preparation for the many studies of Mlle. Gilot that he was going to make with his brush did he venture to touch.

Mlle. Gilot was induced to move into Picasso's studio, and thenceforth was rather at his mercy, though by and large she appears to have succeeded in holding her own. They had all the usual quarrels and estrangements which such a relationship involves, and in the end separated, as was inevitable. What we have to be grateful for is the wonderfully clear, perceptive picture of Picasso which the experience of living with him has enabled Mlle. Gilot to provide. A picture of a superstitious, parsimonious, whimsical, maddeningly mischievous and unaccountable gnome of a man, gifted with that inexhaustible fount of vitality which is the necessary and invariable accompaniment of genius. Some of the anecdotes are superb. I like particularly the account of a visit to a bullfight, and the truly hilarious attempt to get invited to luncheon with Braque.

To one reader at any rate, far from denigrating Picasso, Mlle. Gilot for the first time makes him human, comprehensible and even admirable. The boring, unconvincing hero of abstract painting, the equally unconvincing saint and sage of mid-twentieth-century communism, becomes an inspired and intrepid joker who will send an art dealer to London to buy him a hat; who gleefully enjoys the spectacle of the prime targets of his grotesques paying out vast sums for them; and who has a clear, ironical awareness of the artistic cul-de-sac in which he finds himself. Mlle. Gilot describes Picasso working away at the Musée d'Antibes; a place I have visited several times, grieving over the decay, as it seemed to me, of a great talent there manifest. I shall grieve no longer. Thanks to Mlle. Gilot, henceforth I shall see the later Picasso as monkeyish rather than senile, a gargoyle rather than an abyss.

'The thing that's wrong with modern art,' Mlle. Gilot quotes him as saying, 'and we might as well say it - it's dying - is the fact that there isn't any longer a strong, powerful academic art worth fighting against. There has to be a rule even if it's a bad one because the evidence of art's power is in breaking down the barriers. But to do away with obstacles - that serves no purpose other than to make things completely wishy-washy, spineless, shapeless, meaningless - zero.' He said it, and he ought to know.

Edmund Wilson's expanded version of his *The Scrolls from the Dead Sea*, published in 1955 (*The Dead Sea Scrolls, 1947-1969*) is, as usual, a pleasure to read. Other writers on this fascinating subject may, for all I know, be more expert and learned than he, but none whose work I have looked at come anywhere near equalling him in clarity and ease of narrative and exposition. The non-scientific and unlearned like myself suffer acutely from the atrocious prose in which sociologists, anthropologists and other such write. What a joy, then, to have Mr Wilson for a guide in a field that all to easily lends itself to pedantry and obscurity!

The story of the discovery of the Dead Sea Scrolls is now, I should suppose, sufficiently well known. How some Arab boys playing in a cave near the Dead Sea came upon some pots which seemed unusual enough for them to take away and offer for sale. How after much coming and going, complicated by the breaking out of one of the recurrent Arab-Israel wars, it was discovered that these pots contained fragments of manuscripts which once constituted the library of a community of ascetics in that neighbourhood at the time of Christ, probably known as Essenes, though not so described in the manuscripts themselves. How in due course scholars were able to piece the manuscripts together, finding therein texts of the Hebrew scriptures and Psalms, as well as a detailed and exact account of the communities rule and way of life.

As it happens, some eighteen months ago I saw the place where this momentous discovery was made, and was awed by the sight of some of the manuscripts so brilliantly displayed in the Shrine of the Book near the Hebrew University. I also spent some time listening to Professor David Flusser's tempestuous outpouring of words, just as Mr Wilson describes it, and had the privilege of being taken round the relevant sites by Père Benoit, director of the École Biblique in Jerusalem, where so much work on the Scrolls – notably by Père de Vaux – has been done. Thus for me Mr Wilson's book had a particular interest and gave particular delight.

An essential element in the doctrine of the Dead Sea community is the notion of there being two opposing ways – a way of Darkness and a Way of Light, Darkness being Falsehood and Light Truth. The Messiah, or teacher of Righteousness, belongs to the Way of light which leads to salvation; the Demon, more frequently called Belial or Beliar, belongs to the Way of Darkness which leads to torment. A Last Judgement is foretold when the Messiah divides the world, and His people, the Elect, are saved and the wrongs they have suffered at the hands of their enemies avenged. Until this happens they must keep themselves holy by means of sacred repasts presided over by a priest and by purification through baptism. In the course of describing all this, Mr Wilson points out, there are three references to 'living water' which recall the conversation recorded in the Gospels between Jesus and the woman of Samaria at the well when He speaks of the 'spring of water welling up to eternal life.' The concept of water as an image of spiritual regeneration is of course expressed in the practice of Christian baptism; Mr Wilson quotes a remarkable passage from the Dead Sea community's Manual of Discipline which expresses the same concept: 'sprinkling upon him a Spirit of truth as purifying water to cleanse him from all untrue abominations and from wallowing in the spirit of impurity, so as to give the upright insight into the knowledge of the Most

High and into the wisdom of the sons of Heaven, to give the perfect way of understanding.'

Such similarities between the Scrolls and the New Testament have been taken as implying that Jesus was strongly influenced by this Dead Sea community flourishing in his time, though there is no reference to it in the Gospel, nor to him in the Scrolls. It has even been suggested that John the Baptist, and perhaps Jesus Himself, may have been for a while members of the community. In John the Baptist's case this is possible but unlikely; in Jesus' case highly improbable. Even if it were so, I cannot myself see that it would make any essential difference to the validity of Jesus' life and teaching, or to the Christian hope of salvation that He lived and died to proclaim.

The historicity of the Gospels, as it seems to me, is something quite distinct from their truth. As myths might be true, and as history false. This is a proposition that many Christians, and not only fundamentalists, would find highly distasteful. These look with some apprehension at the unfolding testimony of the Scrolls, and dread, I dare say, that discoveries may be made casting doubt on essential incidents like the Resurrection or Jesus' miraculous birth. They might even be troubled by the knockabout turns of Dr. John Allegro of Manchester University, one of the experts engaged in unravelling the Scrolls, who, as Mr Wilson shows, has been responsible for some of the wilder claims on their behalf - as that 'the names of Jesus and all the Apostles, including Judas, are disguises for the titles of Essene officials, and that...the members of the Sect were 'diviners' as well as healers and the Gospels a 'handbook of witchcraft." Mr Wilson rightly compares such outlandish fancies with the search for hidden ciphers in Shakespeare's plays. Dr Allegro's latest suggestion, it seems, is that it is possible to trace the roots of Christianity to 'a phallic, drug-taking mystery cult,' and the prophets were on LSD 'or something very like it. They *had* visions, they were on a trip.'

Such wild suggestions are only, it seems to me, carrying to its reducto ad absurdom the search for historical truth in the Gospels. In fact, Jesus was as far beyond history as truth is beyond knowledge. One may forage about in history indefinitely, always discovering new slants and re-evaluating the great figures of the past. For everything in time, the perspective changes; we see yesterday differently in the light of today, and then, when today has become yesterday, it, too, is seen differently. All in time is shifting; there can be no fixed history. Reputations rise and fall, the pattern is broken and then reformed. If Jesus is taken into history, then He must partake of this shifting quality of time, and the Christian faith becomes not everlasting truth, but another ideology, seen thus at such a time and thus at another, valid perhaps yesterday, but invalid today and forgotten tomorrow.

Where, then, I ask myself, does the truth of Jesus and his message lie if not in history? One may glimpse the answer in art and literature, which, however insecurely, exists beyond time as history does not. Thus Shakespeare's Caesar is more like Caesar than Caesar was, and the vision of a Blake reaches into regions which no astronaut will ever explore. We today are imprisoned in history as few generations, if any, have ever been because we only believe in the dimensions of time and the certainty of fact. We have science and no art, sociology and no literature, the Dead Sea Scrolls and no Gospel, Jesus and no Christ.

⊬⊷⊣

In the crack up of a civilisation, as of an individual, there is inevitably a strong element of masquerade. The drunk in the old *Punch* drawings puts on his wife's hat, or shakes hand with a lamppost. In the same sort of way, our Western societies lurch and reel toward dissolution to the accompaniment of Marx Brothers-type farce, provided, to a great extent, by the so-called kids, or students. (I say 'so called' because, more often than not, the leading role is taken by figures well into their thirties whose student days, if they ever had any, are well behind them.) A favourite scene for such macabre frolics is a court of law, and of course, the media, especially television, ensure the widest possible diffusion. Thus, for instance, the recent proceedings in Chicago against the alleged inciters of the disturbances there at the time of the Democratic Convention that nominated Hubert Humphrey, have had an exceptionally high rating, and their possibilities in the way of public entertainment are by no means yet exhausted.

In this particular case, Judge Julius Hoffman put on as good a funny turn as any of the eight defendants, but for my money the most side-splitting element of all in such affairs is not so much the actual performers as the totally solemn commentator who purports to see in the harlequinade the working out of some tremendous sociological or historical destiny, the superior fall guy who finds, as it were, a *King Lear* theme in the preposterous clowning of the mechanicals in

129

Midsummer Nights Dream. Here, a high place in the straw-in-the-hair stakes must be awarded to Jason Epstein, (*The Great Conspiracy Trial*) a scion of the House of Random and a pillar of *The New York Review of Books,* both citadels of Radical Chic. (I thank thee Tom Wolfe for teaching me that phrase!) Though no kid himself, Epstein describes the ribald Chicago proceedings with a portentousness, a concentration of moral indignation, which Gladstone might have envied when he denounced the Bulgarian atrocities, or William Jennings Bryan when he expatiated upon the appalling consequences of teaching the theory of evolution in Tennessee.

On this side of the Atlantic we have, as a matter of fact, been to some extent conditioned for the Epstein treatment by a massive televised dramatisation of the trial in question by the BBC – itself a great engine of righteousness in such matters. At the same time, thanks to a visit by one of the defendants – Jerry Rubin – and his appearance along with some of his entourage, on the English version of *The David Frost Show,* we have been able to see at first hand something of the routines which brought the house down again and again in Chicago. These consisted, for the most part, of shouting obscenities, squirting a water pistol, smoking pot and calling Frost a plastic man – this last point, as I thought, though true enough, somewhat scurvily put, in that it was Frost's plasticity which got Rubin and his mates onto the show at all. In Chicago, with Judge Hoffman for Frost, it required a whole plastic legal system to procure exposure for him.

How far the happening was unforeseen, as Frost claimed, is open to doubt, especially as a second studio proved to be miraculously available and in working order when the Rubin gang's antics had got out of hand.

In any case, their turbulent behaviour could have been anticipated by anyone who has read Rubin's own offering (*Do It!*) in which he explains just how important television is to a kid revolutionary. Let me add that *DO IT!* is as refreshing a change after *The Great Conspiracy Trial* as an encounter with the Artful Dodger after an evening with Mr Podsnap.

The difficulty with the Epstein approach is that its two purposes are contradictory. The kids must be regarded either as revolutionary associates of the Black Panthers, in which case the accusations made against them in Chicago were substantially correct, or as peaceable demonstrators with no subversive intent, in which case they are not revolutionaries. Epstein's thesis requires them to be both. Thus, for instance, Bobby Seal, the Black Panther leader indicted along with Rubin and the others, has to appear as a Che Guevara and a Martin Luther King Jr, all in one. His words must be as a clarion call to the barricades and as blameless as a triolet. Even Mr Epstein finds this rather hard going. It is not easy, on any showing, to detect the cooing of a dove in pronouncements like: 'If a pig comes up to us unjustly, we should bring out our pieces and start barbecuing that pork, and if they get in our way, we should kill some of those pigs and put them on a morgue slab.'

Another of the defendants at the Chicago proceedings, Tom Haydon (*Trial*) has provided an account of them. It is much shorter than Mr Epstein's, more discursive and confused, but I still somehow prefer it, as I prefer the roughest Cheddar to anything processed. Hayden, it seems, was one of the founders of Students for a Democratic Society, and has played a leading part in student turbulence. He, too, is an ageing kid. The trial, as he sees it, is just one more manifestation of the struggle that is going on between the forces of revolutionary change and the entrenched Establishment, between young and the old, between pot and cigar smokers; between the fuzz whose murderous bullets are 'unleashed against tender white skin' and the wearers of the tender white skin – the liberated Yippees who have reversed the Fall, sicked up the forbidden apple, and returned to the Garden of Eden, where they summon us all to live.

At the same time, Hayden is assailed with doubts about the consequences of the Chicago trial to its leading participants, of whom, of course, he is one. His personal relationships, he says, shrivelled to nothing during its course. At weekends he would return to Berkley to refresh himself, and then, on Monday morning, 'drop a pill...to turn on the production machine again.' He goes on: 'Our male chauvinism, elitism, and egotism were merely symptoms of the original problem – the Movement did not choose us to be its symbols; the press and government did.' Only males with driving egos can hope to 'rise in the Movement or rock culture and be accepted by the media and dealt with seriously by the Establishment.' In other words, in addition to all his other grievances about the bullets in the tender flesh, and Judge Hoffman, and the 'special task forces established in the Justice Department to go after the Panthers and other groups,' etc, etc, Hayden has this additional one – that the Establishment will insist on showering its blessings on his reluctant head.

So, he finds, you begin to make contacts and contracts, you get $1,000 per speech, you are sought after for television appearances. Random House - and he sees it as a decidedly sinister circumstance - 'not only published *Woodstock Nation;* it takes part in the put-on with a cover illustration in which its trademark building is shown being blown up.' Simon & Scchuster likewise offend by advertising Rubin's book, with his approval as 'a Molotov cocktail in your very hands,' as '*The Communist Manifesto* of our era.' I agree it is disconcerting. Doesn't it mean, Hayden asks, that 'the corporate executives and advertisers sense something familiar and manageable in this revolution?' Alas, yes. In the early days of the Labour Party we used to call this the aristocratic embrace. The horny-handed sons of toil whom we sent to Parliament were taken up by duchesses, took to wearing tails and a white tie, collected decorations and were raised to the peerage. With us, it has always been snobbishness rather than money or mere celebrity, but that was before television. Now, maybe, it's cash and the press cuttings here, too.

'At the trial's end,' Hayden woefully discloses, 'we were seriously planning to sell movie rights to big commercial producers, and Abbie [Abbie Hoffman, whose *Revolution For The Hell Of It* was sold to MGM] was declaring, 'Let them have Washington, DC; we're going to take over Hollywood.' So, to a great extent they have, for what it's worth.

⊱──━─⊰

I once asked Norman Mailer why at that time - some five years ago - all the most successful American writers seemed to be Jewish. He said he thought the reason must be that when a traditionally oppressed minority like the Jews achieves a position of social equality, energy and creativity are released in them. On this basis, he expected that quite soon the most successful American writers would be Black. His prophecy has been to a great extent fulfilled. Today, a black writer has much working on his behalf apart from the intrinsic quality of his work - the sense of guilt among his white fellow citizens, for one thing. Literary and other critics are being called in to rectify the villainies of slave traders and the commercial interests they so lavishly benefited.

For my own part, I must say, I find this literature of black *saeva indignatio* very little to my taste. A case in point is the late George L Jackson's *Blood in My Eye*. Like *Soul On Ice* and *The Autobiography of Malcolm X*, for that matter like Jackson's own previous volume, *Soledad Brother*, I find it somehow synthetic and processed. Whether such books are in fact worked on by other hands, put through an editorial sausage machine, or just reflect the stereotypes of Black American revolt, I cannot tell. I suspect the former. The very terms in which they are hailed follow a well-worn pattern, and would be considered excessive if applied to Aristotle, Thomas Aquinas and Eric Sevareid rolled into one. Gregory Armstrong, who contributes a Preface to *Blood in My Eye*, limits himself, it is true, to claiming that Jackson's 'Marxian economics and history rivalled that of most college professors' - which, after all, isn't saying much, if anything. Otherwise, he conveys a picture of such heroic dimensions, such sublimity of thought and action, that it quite fails to convince. Incidentally, he spells America with a 'K', as is the usage throughout the book, which I take to be some mystical way of indicating that Washington, Jefferson, Lincoln and Co. had very little to do with the destiny, manifest or otherwise, of the nation they thought they were founding.

This is not to show any lack of sympathy with Jackson; the poor fellow spent most of his life in prison, and died in a fracas in which he may or may not have been the aggressor. The precise reasons for his long detention and circumstances of his death will probably now never be known. He has become part of the contemporary legend, and must, like Che Guevara and Malcolm X, be forever a subject of controversy as to whether he was the blameless victim of white racialist arrogance, or the black hoodlum who applied the same instincts which made him a criminal into being a revolutionary ideologue. Nothing, it is safe to say, in *Blood in My Eye*, will clear up the point. Jackson's political theorizing has a very jejune flavour about it, and rings as falsely as the amiable liberal sentiments associated with Uncle Tom. In fact, *Comrade Tom's Revolution* might almost provide an alternative title.

The book, as is usual in the genre, proves too much. For instance, if the conditions in prison were so appalling, a sane reader (assuming there are any such) must ask himself how it came about that Jackson was able to study and write, get access to books and stationery, make tapes of his dissertations and proclamations and distribute them, receive the press and give interviews, etc. Again, if it was so inconceivable that Jackson could have killed anybody, why the constant exhortations to kill. For instance:

'There are many thousands of ways to correct individuals. The best way is to send one armed expert. I don't mean to outshout him with logic, I mean correct him. Slay him, assassinate him with thuggee, by silenced pistol, shotgun, with a high-powered rifle shooting from four hundred yards away and behind a rock. Suffocation, strangulation, crucifixion, burning with flamethrower, dispatch by bomb. Auto accidents happen all day. People drown, get pole-axed, breathe noxious gases, get stabbed, get poisoned with bad water, ratsbane, germicides, hemlock, arsenic, strychnine, LSD 25 concentrate, cyanide, hydrocyanic acid, vitriol. A snake could bite him, nicotine oil is deadly, an overdose of dope; there's deadly nightshade, belladonna, datura, wolfsbane, foxglove, aconite, ptomaine, botulism, and the death of a thousand cuts. But a curse won't work.'

This, I think it will be agreed, is scarcely reminiscent of the Sermon on the Mount, and there are plenty of other passages in a similar vein. They do not, however, at all abate the ardour of Jackson's champions in asserting that so gentle, poetic and loving a man would in no circumstances be capable of the crimes of violence attributed to him.

It seems to me that there is a contradiction here, and one that runs through all apologias for black intransigence. Thus, in his address at a memorial service for Jackson, the Black Panther leader Huey Newton pledged himself and his followers to 'take the example from George Jackson,' and 'in the name of love and in the name of freedom, with love as our guide, we'll slit every throat of anyone who threatens the people and our children. We'll do it in the name of peace . . .' Orwell, who delighted in his concept of a Ministry of Love making war, and a Ministry of Truth fabricating lies, would have enjoyed Newton's line of thought, arguing, I daresay, that, though his passion to kill might be justified, or at any rate understood, it was surely rather farfetched to see it as a manifestation of love, a cry for freedom and peace.

⁘

Professor Passmore's fascinating exploration of the quest for perfection during the last 3,000 tears (*The Perfectibility of Man,* by John Passmore) takes us from Homer's Olympus, through Plato, Pelagius and the Enlightenment, HG Wells and the hipster communes of California. Perfectibility is, as he shows, the great will-o'- the-wisp of human life, productive of some of Mankind's more outstanding achievements, as well as some of its more outrageous follies.

No one, I should have thought, looking honestly into his own heart, could suppose himself capable of attaining perfection in any field or in any respect. The Christian doctrine of Original Sin is thus a more comfortable preposition than perfectibility. Likewise the most superficial study of history would, one might suppose, put paid to any notion of collective perfection: for instance a perfect society, or a perfect educational system.

None the less, the quest goes on; the more ardently, it seems sometimes, when, as today, every circumstance points inexorably the other way. Pacifists pick themselves up from the rubble of two monstrously destructive wars to proclaim yet again their faith in the coming of a reign of everlasting peace. Marxist freedom-lovers, after learning about Stalin's enormities, avert their eyes from the Kremlin only to fix them with renewed hope on Peking or Havana. And so on. If, as I often suppose, the divine plan is to cure us of entertaining hopes of earthly perfection by demonstrating ever more dramatically their futility, then clearly, the lesson remains unlearnt. The last half century, on any showing, has been notable for demonstrating human inadequacy to a quite exceptional degree; it has also been unusually prolific in prospectuses for various kinds of instant paradise.

Professor Passmore works over this outlandish material with grace and skill. He carries a large load of erudition lightly; his own attitude of detachment and careful moderation suits his theme perfectly. Like Gibbon, he manages to infuse his sentences with a pleasant flavour of irony without seeming to be unduly censorious or contemptuous of the absurdities he so often has to recount. His own conclusions are philosophical. 'Perfection,' he writes, 'is no more to be expected from the destruction of existing social institutions than from their extension and strengthening. The chains which men bear they have imposed on themselves; strike them off, and they will weep for their lost security.'

The pagan gods, he points out, were themselves imperfect, and Plato's perfectionist hopes were centred on an élite, not on the generality of mankind. Christianity, as it were, brought the extras on to the stage in addition to the stars, though initially it was a strongly anti-perfectionist faith. After all, most of St Paul's first converts were slaves who, by virtue of their very condition, felt little inclination to envisage participation in a perfect human society on earth. Also, their new faith required them to believe in the imminence of a Second Coming and the millennium, which automatically, for obvious reasons, ruled out any serious concern with short-term Utopian projects. It is interesting to reflect that these two

circumstances, which might normally be regarded as disad-
vantageous - the preponderance of slaves in the first Christian
congregations and the mistaken belief that the world would
soon end - proved in practice a great asset. Apocalypticism
is a far less dangerous error than utopianism. To believe in
the forthcoming end of the world wonderfully concentrates
the mind, as Dr Johnson said of being condemned to death,
whereas to believe that mortal men can create a lasting heav-
en is a an absurdity which opens the mind to every variety off
folly and dishonesty.

Christians, however, as Professor Passmore shows, soon began to ask themselves whether, when they were told to be
perfect 'even as your Father which is in Heaven is perfect,' this
was meant literally. Perhaps significantly, it was an Englishman
- Pelagius - who insisted that it was. God, he contended, 'has
not willed to command anything impossible, for He is right-
eous; and He will not condemn a man for what he could not
help, for He is holy.' Pelagius's chief antagonist, who ultimately
demolished him, was Augustine, but the Pelagian heresy lived
on to produce in his native land some 15 centuries later an
amazing crop of freedom-fighting, family-planning, guitar-
twanging clerics the like of whom had never before been
seen on earth.

If Christianity contributed powerful commandos to the
perfectionist forces, the big battalions, the heavy armour and
the atomic weaponry came from science. Here Professor Passmore has a wonderful time indeed. Darwinism lent itself to
the ultimate extravagances of perfectionism; if homo sapiens
represented the pinnacle of the evolutionary process, what
glories might lie just round the corner as this chosen species

went on evolving! The doctrine of progress – certainly the most foolish, possibly the most deleterious, ever to be entertained – suggested that change itself, if suitably supported, must always lead to perfection. All that was required was that we should coast along on the tide of our own hopes and desires, and then, infallibly, we should be carried into the harbour of the Heavenly City, there to land and live happily ever after.

The early contributors to this fantasy – the Darwins, the Huxleys, the Herbert Spencers and Karl Marxes even – might be considered as being relatively rational and in possession of their right minds; the last inheritors of it in our own time – the HG Wells, the Marcuses, the Marshal McLuhans and Timothy Learys – as deviating totally from sense. Like Doeg in *Absalom and Achitophel*

'Through Sense and Non-sense, never out nor in;

Free from all meaning, whether good or bad;

And in one word. Heroically mad'

So, in due course, I foresee an epilogue to Professor Passmore's excellent book, describing how, as faith in perfectibility augmented, the ways and works of men grew ever more imperfect, until, making one last reach in the direction of their own health, wealth and happiness, the darkness fell upon them and their world. Meanwhile, we can make do with the narrative as far as Professor Passmore has taken it, noting his own moderate conclusion that, though Man's passions are useless if they induce him to see himself as God, they 'are not useless if they help him to become a little more humane, a little more civilised.'

⊹══⊱

The Care of Devils (by Sylvia Press) first made its appearance in 1958, when it fell about as flat as a novel of its competence and topicality possibly can. This I find somewhat surprising in view of the fact that it provides, with a candour and authenticity I have not come across elsewhere, a blow-by-blow account of the interrogation of a suspected subversive in an American intelligence agency – clearly the CIA – during the ill-omened McCarthy era. Apart from any other consideration, *The Care of Devils* would seem to me to be of major interest as documentation. It contains, for instance, the only first-hand description I have ever read of what it is like to be harnessed to the ridiculous polygraph, or lie-detector machine – a contraption so redolent of the particular imbecility of this age, with its obsessive belief that everything, including ultimately fornication, can be set up and operated mechanically. Considered just as fiction, *The Care of Devils* is no masterpiece, but well above the average of many novels which make a big stir in the women's clubs; as a piece of social history, I found it impressive – vivid, informative, and obviously sincere.

The dust jacket informs us that the authoress, Miss Sylvia Press, was 'for many years an American intelligence officer here and abroad.' It thus may be assumed that she and her heroine, Ellen Simon, are approximately one and the same person. Her novel obviously would not have been pleasing – in fact, highly distasteful – to the CIA and its then boss, Allen Dulles, whose views on the necessity of confirming that intelligence officers remain 'clean as a whistle' by means of regular interrogations, fortified by the use of the polygraph, have been stated publicly. The question naturally arises in one's mind, therefore, as to whether the Agency may not have taken a hand in ensuring that Miss Press's novel was kept off the bookstands.

My own consciousness of the ineptitude and incompetence of publishers is that I require no theory of outside interference to account for the failure of any novel. On the other hand, I know from experience that intelligence organizations are capable of any folly. As between the incompetence of publishers and the folly of intelligence organizations, I am neutral, and content myself with stating what seems to me to be incontrovertible - *viz.*, that Miss Press's novel deals with matters of great and, alas, continuing importance, in an interesting and, as far as one can judge, truthful manner, and that nonetheless it seems to have largely escaped the notice of booksellers, book buyers and reviewers alike.

In the last respect, at least, I can belatedly try and mend matters. The story begins with the heroine, Ellen, at work in the Washington headquarters of the CIA. She is clearly a fairly senior and experienced officer, with an assistant of her own. She has worked overseas, we are given to understand, having been recruited into the Agency in the war years when it was the OSS (Ah, those first OSS arrivals in London! How well I remember them - arriving like *jeunes filles en fleur* straight from a finishing school, all fresh and innocent, to start work in our frowsty old intelligence brothel! All too soon they were ravished and corrupted, becoming indistinguishable from seasoned pros who had been in the game for a quarter of a century and more.) Ellen's current problem is to decide on

the bona fides or otherwise of a defector from the Communists – a problem of whose complexity only those who have
had to handle it will be aware; the truth being that the great
majority of defectors are actuated by interested, rather than
idealistic or ideological motives – money, a girl, that sort of
thing – so that, as one is uneasily aware, should the balance
of advantage swing the other way, they would be liable to
redefect, and in that sense cannot ever be regarded as reliable.

Ellen is convinced – as it turns out, rightly – that her man is
a phoney, a point which crops up several times in the course
of the narrative. The suggestion seems to be that Ellen's discovery of the man's phoneyness is a point against her rather
than for her; almost as though her superiors had a stake in
his genuineness, resented his exposure, and took out their
annoyance on Ellen. In the conditions of panic created by
McCarthy in government agencies this is perfectly possible, especially if the defector in question had been somehow
sponsored by the Wisconsin Senator's ribald entourage. Such
situations, in any case, are all too liable to arise in intelligence
organizations the world over, all of them being abnormally
subject to internecine conflict. I know of a case in the war
of a very valuable source of information remaining unused
because the man who turned it up happened to be personally
disliked by a senior officer at headquarters. Again, there is the
case of Cicero, the British Ambassador in Ankara's valet, who
extracted from the Embassy safe the full plans and order of
battle for the invasion of France and sold them, as it turned
out for counterfeit money, to the Abwehr. Himmler was so
furious at a rival organization's pulling off this coup that he
arranged for the documents to be pigeonholed and never

passed to the military. I often used to reflect, when I was an intelligence officer, that if only we could concentrate on the enemy the insensate hatred we directed at one another, the war would be won in no time.

While still grappling with the problem of the defector, Ellen is called away to the Internal security Department, where, to her amazement and chagrin, she discovers that she is a suspect herself. Then there begins a long, exhausting and distressing process of interrogation, day after day, week after week, in which the whole of Ellen's life, her love affairs, her friend-ships, every tiny detail and nuance of her private existence are gone into by her two clottish interrogators. The interest and suspense are well maintained, as is the sense, almost over-whelming at times, of the unspeakable disgustingness of the whole procedure. Ellen, of course, as soon as she realized what was afoot, should have slapped her interrogators in the face for their impertinent curiosity, scattered their precious dossi-ers about the floor, and otherwise manifested her contempt for them and all their ridiculous, dog-eared tricks - the light shining in her face, the dark mentions of knowing more than they say, the elaborately staged confrontation, etc., etc. Then, with a sigh of relief, she should have got herself a job as a bar-tender or call girl, something nice and wholesome and fresh, and lived happily ever after. In America and the countries of the West we can still do this; in the USSR they cannot. It is one of the few remaining dividends of what we like to call our free way of life.

Actually, Ellen does nothing of the sort. Racked by anxiety, sleepless, distracted, she endures the humiliating procedure, tries desperately to prove her innocence - though without knowing what she is being accused of – searches through old papers and letters, goes over and over in her mind just what happened on such an occasion, what was said, who was present. She is a willing victim, and could not really be expected to be otherwise. After all, she is in the métier. She has lost her right to protest because she has participated in subjecting others to similar treatment. She, too, has framed the idiot questions, done the idiot research, taken the unpardonable liberty of violating that essential integrity of the person whose safeguarding is the basis of all civilization. The savage is vulnerable to the tribe; the civilized man may proudly claim that as long as he obeys certain specified and known laws, whose contravention carries equally specified penalties, his life is his own. The moment the state allows probing fingers to be intruded there, then barbarism has set in.

Poor Ellen has relinquished her own rights by virtue of her occupation. She has touched pitch, and now is being tarred herself. There she sits, relentlessly being questioned by two fellow Americans about all sorts of matters which have nothing whatever to do with them, or with the CIA, or the United States Government; matters which pertain to herself alone, and can be broached only in the intimacy of love or the ecstasy of faith – in bed or in the confessional. It is terrible to think of such things going on in the shadow of the Lincoln Memorial – procedures and practices which are a denial of everything that our history, our religion, our literature and our traditions are supposed to cherish.

People forget that it has all happened so recently. I can just remember my father, before the 1914–18 war, going abroad. For money he had golden sovereigns which were acceptable everywhere; he did not need to take with him a single document. The only country where passports were required was – how significant – Russia. In what is often regarded now as the unenlightened nineteenth century, anyone could come to England who wanted to. To quote the opening sentences of A.J.P. Taylor's brilliant volume in The Oxford History of England (*English History 1914 - 1945*):

'Until August 1914 a sensible, law–abiding Englishman could pass through life and hardly notice the existence of the state, beyond the post office and the policeman. He could live where he liked and how he liked and as he liked. He had no official number or identity card. He could travel abroad or leave his country forever without a passport or any sort of official permission. He could exchange his money for any other money without restriction or limit. He could buy goods from any country in the world on the same terms as he bought goods at home. For that matter, a foreigner could spend his life in this country without permit and without informing the police.'

London was full of subversives of every sort and description – anarchists, Communists, crackpots, Karl Marx in person – all busily plotting the overthrow of our and every other government in the world. At the same time, the United States was growing into the richest and most powerful nation on earth by similarly allowing everyone who had a mind to cross the Atlantic to come to New York to try their luck. Did people in those days wake up trembling lest subversives had got into the Home Office, or some diplomat of ours be contemplating defecting to another country? Not at all. Everything suggests that they slept in their beds a good deal more quietly than

we do, though MI5 consisted then of at most seven elder-
ly retired officers from the Indian Army, whereas today it is
numbered in hundreds and the Secret Service in thousands,
and both organizations together, at a rough estimate, cost the
taxpayer about the equivalent of the total defence budget in
the days of Gladstone. As for America – what the FBI and the
CIA dispose of in the way of manpower and public money,
God alone knows, but it must be astronomical.

At the end of her ordeal Miss Press's heroine is fired as a
security risk. Instead of having a great ball to celebrate this
blessed release, she manages to get admitted to the head man
– presumably Dulles – and begs him at least to tell her what
she has been found guilty of. He murmurs something about
'lack of candour,' but it is obvious that he has not read the
report of her interrogation, and that she is in some sort a
sacrificial victim offered up to appease Senator McCarthy
and his Un-American Activities Committee. Cut off from all
hopes of redress within the CIA, she settles down to write
her own version of the affair. The result is *The Care of Devils*.
Incidentally, I should point out that in England she would
have been denied even this recourse. With our usual cunning
we have devised a splendid instrument for shutting every-
body up without expense or the risk of public scandal. This
is the Official Secrets Act, which requires every employee in
Defence and Intelligence Departments to give an undertaking that he will not disclose any information which comes
to him in the course of his duties upon pain of a fine and/or
a term of imprisonment. Thus, if Miss Press had worked for
British Intelligence she would have been required to submit
the manuscript of *The Care of Devils* to the department she

worked for before it could legally be published. There, we may be sure, it would have come to rest.

The question naturally arises as to whether Ellen was guilty. Had she, in fact, done anything wrong? In the novel, she is constantly putting just this question to herself. It is a perfect Kafka situation; she is accused of nothing, yet is tormented alternately by a sense of guilt and of outraged innocence. Her whole moral fabric is corroded away. If she is guilty she must keep away from her friends lest she contaminate them. Anyway, who are her friends? Has she got any? If so, are they accomplices? Or secret enemies who will be brought out to accuse her? With the most extraordinary prophetic vision, in his novel *The Trial* Kafka foresees that this is going to become the human condition - to be accused of an unknown crime; to be investigated, interrogated, kept under surveillance, pressed to confess, even confessing, perhaps at last executed. Guilty or not guilty? Who can say? Since there is no crime. Only guilt.

Insofar as there was any cogent thought in the sick and vacuous minds of Ellen's interrogators, it was, presumably, that the man - Steve Lasker, with whom Ellen had had a love affair and been on a trip to Mexico - had some sort of bad security record which contaminated her. Let us assume the worst - that Lasker had been a Soviet agent, that Ellen in retrospect had vague suspicions of him, and that, because he had been her lover, consciously or unconsciously, she wanted to shield him, and so was sometimes evasive and less than candid in answering questions about their relationship. Is this really so very reprehensible? It is, in any case, a matter which could have been settled honestly and honorably in five minutes by just putting the point to Ellen. This was never done. It was skirted round, hinted at, touched upon, but never put. Right up to the end, and afterward, she had no means of knowing what, if anything, they had against Lasker. Nor, rather surprisingly, did she apparently make any effort, then or subsequently, to seek out Lasker and have it out with him. The central character in the melodrama is never brought onto the stage, perhaps because, if he were to be, the melodrama would turn into farce - which, in a sort of way, Ellen wanted no more than her interrogators did.

It will surely strike future historians as strange that we, who talk endlessly about freedom, who have drenched the world in blood and destruction to liberate so-called captive peoples, who look with a baleful eye at the nightmare of Stalin's purges, should yet see fit, in the alleged interest of security, to subvert our own ostensibly prized liberties. In the eyes of posterity it will inevitably seem that, in safeguarding our freedom, we destroyed it; that the vast clandestine apparatus we built up to probe our enemies' resources and intentions only served in the end to confuse our own purposes; that the practice of deceiving others for the good of the state led infallibly to our deceiving ourselves, and that the vast army of Intelligence personnel built up to execute these purposes were soon caught up in the web of their own sick fantasies, with disastrous consequences to them and us.

Miss Press's novel is an excellent antidote to the Bond books, which delight Intelligence pros, as they dazzle the general public, by making an intrinsically sinister and sordid activity seem glamorous, exciting and honourable. *The Care of Devils* has precisely the opposite effect. Through the characterization of her heroine, herself in the web, and through the manner of her ejection from it, Miss Press shows how an organization like the CIA really works, and what it is about.

The Care of Devils will assuredly *not* please the pros. From their point of view it has the truly appalling disability of being true.

+≒≒+

A favourite contemporary illusion is that the only virtuous and interesting people in the world are whores, thieves, junkies, perverts, liars, cheats, and others that used to be considered undesirable characters. On this basis, criminals have a special claim to be regarded with sympathy, if not admiration, and those whose business it is to deal with them - judges, police, prison warders, etc., etc. - become the particular targets of contempt and derision. My own experience, such as it is, suggests the contrary. I have found the conversation of whores even more tedious than that of female dons (whom in some respects they resemble), and criminals I have known have one and all been notable for their insatiable conceit and propensity for lying. However, the public taste points in an opposite direction, and a considerable literature has grown up designed to exemplify the moral, spiritual and intellectual excellence of the criminal classes.

A classic in this *genre* is Henri Charrière's *Papillon* which, we are told, has already sold a million copies in the French edition, and is now offered in English, in a translation by Mr Patrick O'Brian. It is an account of M. Charrière's experiences ('Papillon' was his underworld *nom-de-crime*) in prison in French Guiana and Devil's Island; of his various attempted escapes, and ultimate liberation to literary stardom and the affluence that goes therewith.

GK Chesterton once remarked that the lights of Broadway would look marvellous if only one couldn't read. Similarly, I might say of *Papillon* that it would make marvellous reading if only I believed it. Alas, I don't. Like other such exercises in self-appreciation – Casanova's *Memoirs*, for instance, or Frank Harris's *My Life and Loves* – it leaves me with an unbridgeable credulity gap. However, a proneness to fantasy is no obstacle to literary repute. Witness TE Lawrence. M. Francois Mauriac finds *Papillon* true, and 'a good book in the deep meaning of the word.' So, like Genet, M. Charrière has a sponsor of impeccable credentials.

In 1931, M. Charrière was convicted of murdering a ponce and sentenced to penal servitude for life. M. Charrière is insistent that the evidence offered by the police was perjured; that the public prosecutor was a malignant brute, and that the jury were '12 bastards brought up to Paris from some perishing village in the country . . . small shopkeepers, pensioners, tradesmen' who couldn't possibly 'understand the life you lead in Montmartre or what it's like to be 25.' It is significant that no one in M. Charrière's narrative who, in conventional terms, could be regarded as respectable, has a good word said for him or her, with the exception of an occasional bishop, priest, nun or Salvation Army worker. There are also some lepers who meet with approval, but they perhaps compensate for their respectability by the disfigurements of their disease.

It is not difficult to see why a 'good old curé' gets a honourable mention. As a result of reciting 'Our father which art in heaven . . .' together, M. Charrière's eyes filled with tears. 'The dear priest saw them and with his plump finger he gathered a big drop as it ran down my cheek. He put it in his mouth and drank it.' This amiable gesture led to the following exchange:-

"How long is it since you wept?'

'Fourteen years.'

'Why 14 years ago?'

'It was the day Mum died.'

He took my hand in his and said: 'Forgive those who have made you suffer so.''

Such sentimentality, combined - as is invariably the case - with a total absence of humour, gives the book a syrupy flavour. At the same time, the notion that Papillon's misdemeanours and the punishment they brought him are entirely due to the machinations of others, is highly acceptable. It relieves him of any sense of guilt, and allows the rest of us the luxury of wallowing in a sense of collective wickedness about which we are not called on to do anything except publicly beat our breasts. Everyone is virtuous because everyone is guilty. The same thing was noticeable in the reception of the television programme 'Cathy Come Home.' Cathy's misfortunes, like Papillon's were seen as resulting from circumstances beyond her control. It so happened that a televised version of Tolstoy's 'Resurrection' was being shown at the same time. Here, too, a woman was victim of social injustice, but because Tolstoy was a great artist and Christian it was made clear, additionally, that every human soul, however wronged, carries a private burden or moral responsibility, and is vested with the hope of moral regeneration.

One may be grateful that M. Charrière, unlike Genet, eschews any account of his erotic life while in prison. On the other hand, he exceeds Genet in his descriptions of violence on the part of warders and of the prisoners among themselves. His adventures while on the run are wild and wonderful indeed, and should provide good material for a film script in due course. I liked particularly his experiences with a tribe of Indians who – need I say it? – in their artless goodness and simplicity put to shame the pretensions of more civilised and sophisticated folk. He was fortunate enough to acquire the affection of two of the female Indians – Lali and Zoraima – both of whom he left pregnant on his departure: 'Farewell, Lali and Zoraima, you incomparable women, so spontaneous and uncalculating, with your reactions so close to nature – at the moment of parting they simply swept all the pearls in the hut into a little linen bag for me.'

In such idyllic circumstances who will question his conclusion that the Indians' wild, savage way of living and protecting themselves taught him something very important for the future – 'that it was better to be an untamed Indian than a legal official with a degree'?

M. Charrière's last escape involved his simulating madness in order to get sent to the asylum. One of the devices he adopted was, when the tub of evening soup was brought in, to go over to it and urinate in it. This, he says, 'cast something of a damper on the room,' which one can well believe. His efforts were successful; he was certified a mental case, and managed thereafter to make off. His final refuge was Venezuela, to whose 'humble fishermen, intellectuals, soldiers and others' *Papillon* is dedicated. It is the measure of M. Charrière's stupendous egotism that the 1939–45 war, which coincided with some of his more striking adventures, by comparison scarcely interested him at all.

Mr O'Brian, not unnaturally, considers *Papillon* to be a literary masterpiece which has developed a new style of oral prose – a 'sunlit, rather husky southern voice that you can listen to for hours on end.' He also considers the book to be 'a furious protest against a society that can for its own convenience shut human beings up in dim concrete cells with bars only at the top, there to live in total silence upon a starvation diet until they are tamed, driven mad or physically destroyed.' What the book does not offer is any sort of suggestion as to what should be done about the Papillons of society, assuming that it is considered desirable that any sort of social order and standards of behaviour should be maintained

⊢══⊣

13

'IN THE BEGINNING WAS THE WORD'

The true purpose of words is to convey meaning, and when this is perfectly achieved – which happens only rarely even in the case of the greatest practitioners – there is a kind of ecstasy. The very humblest and most obscure of scribblers may experience this in some degree when they have managed to string together words so as to produce a collective impact greater than the sum of their separate impacts. Unfortunately, words can also be used to disguise meaning, as musical notes can be untrue and convey discord instead of harmony. There is *le mot injust* as well as *le mot juste*.

It is all set forth with great cogency in the famous opening passage of the forth Gospel in which the doctrine of the Logos is expounded. In the beginning, we are told, was the Word; creation itself began, not with a deed, but with a Word, which in due course was made flesh and dwelt among us, full of grace and truth, thereby exemplifying the whole creative process in a nutshell – to put flesh on words so that they may live among us, gracefully and truthfully. This is the true writers charter, valid for all users of words, at whatever level, written or spoken. They have to watch out, though, for the satanic or false Logos whereby the Word dwells among us, graceless and full of falsity. The words we write and speak and think, are as subject to pollution as the air we breath, the water we drink and the food we eat.

Such word pollution at the present time is particularly strong, and I should say, even more dangerous than other forms of pollution. Polluted air makes us suffocate, polluted water and food make us sick, but polluted words deliver us over to the worst of all fates – to be imprisoned inexorably in fantasy. An iron curtain falls between us and reality. There is hope that the polluted air and water and food may sometime be purified, but once words are polluted they are lost forever, old lexicons are their cemeteries, and turning over the pages is like visiting their graves.

Take, for instance, the word 'love', one of the most beautiful there is. Love is a theme running through the highest flights of literature and art and mysticism; the subject, alike, of the incomparable thirteenth chapter of St Paul's Epistle to the Corinthians, and of poems like Donne's *The Ecstasy*, perhaps the most perfect expression of love between a man and a woman ever to be written. Yet is it not sad to reflect that if I speak of love on any campus between the Berlin Wall and the western seaboard of America, the word will almost certainly be taken as signifying eroticism of one sort or another? In the contemporary estimation, to love is to experience sexual desire, and to make love is to 'have sex'; Dante is elbowed aside to make room for Dr Kinsey, and the beautiful *Genesis* story of Adam and Eve in the Garden of Eden is reduced to the dimensions of *Playboy* magazine. This is not just a case of distorting a words meaning, but of completely altering it, love and lust being no more interchangeable terms than are hunger and greed. Surely the devil must be a philologist!

Inevitably, the Welfare State, the pattern of our English way of life in recent years, has produced its own rare crop of *mot injustes* or verbal fraudulence. Since, by definition, the Welfare State is a kingdom of heaven on earth where everyone is happy and no one is wicked, it follows that any deficiencies in people or in institutions must be due to their circumstances, not to any moral or other inadequacy in them. The categories of Good and Evil, therefore, simply do not exist, any more than they did in the Garden of Eden before the fall. There are problems, which can be solved, but no sins which deserve chastisement. Poverty has been abolished, so there are no poor, only under-privileged. If death has not yet been eliminated, soon it will be; meanwhile, there are terminal cases. As for procreation – where is its sting when there are birth pills to prevent birth and family-planning to prevent families, with remedial abortion to ensure that there are no inexpedient births and remedial euthanasia – called 'mercy-killing' – to ensure that no lives are inexpediently protracted? The Welfare State is an earthly paradise constructed out of words bent to the purpose. Will future social historians, I sometimes ask myself, come upon examples of this strange verbiage accidentally preserved like the Dead Sea Scrolls, and try to make sense of it, reaching the conclusion that it must be related to some esoteric cult whose significance is lost in the mists of time?

The same sort of thing has happened to the key words in politics, as George Orwell has so brilliantly demonstrated in two of his essays: *Politics and the English Language* and *The*

Prevention of Literature and in the passages in *Nineteen Eighty-Four* dealing with Newspeak and devises like *doublethink* and *blackwhite,* whereby the Ministry of Truth carries on the day-to-day manufacture and dissemination of lies, as the corresponding Ministry of Love organises violence and hatred. What Orwell shows with remarkable insight and prescience is that word pollution provides an important adjunct to the establishment and maintenance of authoritarian government, which need not fear subversion when the very words in whose name it takes place - like 'liberation', 'equality', 'democracy' - have been so perverted and falsified that they have lost their true significance and dynamism, being rendered impotent, futile and ultimately ridiculous. By this means, as we have seen, it is perfectly possible to revive slavery in the name of liberation, to institute tyranny in the name of democracy and to enforce privilege in the name of equality - always provided that the requisite words have been suitably processed in advance. Thus we have come to accept People's Democracies in which people have no rights and play no part in choosing their rulers, to acknowledge liberations enforced at gunpoint that effectively abolish all liberty, and to applaud equality and fraternity in terms of an artificially protracted condition of class-war or *soi-disant* cultural revolution. So powerful are words, and so sinister the consequences of allowing them to become polluted.

These are instances of the deliberate pollution of words as part of the operation of power-politics in which the capture of key words like 'freedom' and 'self-determination' and 'majority rule' is the equivalent of taking a crucial fortress or commanding height in military warfare. In battles for men's minds – which is what, ultimately, all wars are about – whoever defines the key words wins.

Word pollution in the context of an ostensibly free society like the countries of Western Europe and the United States, is rather different. In such circumstances meaning can be, as it were, washed away in a great cascade of words– a practice to which demagogues seeking election on a basis of universal franchise commonly resort. Their oratory serves to drown meaning in the same sort of way that in *muzak* the identity of the component tunes is lost in a drooling flow of inchoate musical sound. In his book *Strictly Speaking* Ed Newman, himself a wordsmith of experience and repute, gives some choice examples taken from presidential conventions and other demagogic occasions: 'History will record the greatness of his administration. As it is inscribed upon the permanent page, so it is etched in the minds and hearts of a grateful people... Mr Chairman, I proudly rise tonight to confirm a commitment that was wrought in the crucible of another era... Destiny has again marked this man. A man to match our mountains and our plains.' Even, however, in the field of nomination speeches, normally considered to be impregnably otiose and vacuous, it is possible to trace some shadowy meaning – like poring over the faint markings of an ancient fresco.

It is surely significant that, in his quest for total meaningless, Newman turns, not to politicians in full spate, but to sociologists – specifically Messrs Thomas E. Patterson and Robert D. McLure who made a study of the reaction of voters in the Nixon-McGovern campaign to televised political advertising for the Citizens Research Foundation of Princeton. Their research, Patterson and McLure write, was 'rooted in a specific psychological theory of attitude organisation and change – the attitude belief model developed by Martin Fishbean.' In operating this model, they go on, 'measures of the following variables were obtained during each personal interview wave; issue and candidate image attitudes, beliefs about candidate's issue positions and image characteristics, salience of issues and images, and beliefs about the salience of issues and images to the candidates.' These words may be said over and over, like a surrealist poem without ever catching the tiniest glimpse of coherent thought or meaning. Sociology has given a new dimension to human incoherence.

The quest for incoherence, very notable in contemporary letters, from *Finnigans Wake* to the much admired *Naked Lunch,* is itself a form of word-pollution, and part of the retreat from reality which characterises a civilisation in dissolution. Naturally, this is especially marked in groves of academe, where professors and lecturers gain the favour of students by throwing up an ever denser smokescreen of declamatory words to obscure what are supposed to be their subjects. The great campus pundits of our time all write in strange convoluted sentences, as in this passage, chosen at random from Marcuse's *One Dimensional Man*: 'However, if the socially permitted and encouraged release of libido would be that of partial and localised sexuality, it would be tantamount to an actual compression of erotic energy, and this desublimation would be compatible with the growth of unsublimated as well as sublimated forms of aggressiveness...' When word-pollution reaches such a point as this, that words, far from conveying grace and truth, are just strung together in a pot-pourri of psycho-sociological jargon, becoming a sort of technological mandarin, then surely another Dark Age must be upon us.

To extract meaning from incoherence, order from chaos, harmony from discord – this is what civilisation is about. Meaningful, supple, lucid words are an outward and visible intimation that the secret and invisible civilising process is at work; disorder in words, even more than other forms of disorder, intimates that it has gone into reverse gear. Fiat Nox! replaces Fiat Lux! And the new barbarians shout at their sometime mentors, as Caliban did at Prospero:

'You taught me language; and my profit on't
Is, I know how to curse'.

14

LIE IN THE CAMERA'S EYE

It is now some two decades since I first had the experience of a red-eyed camera closing in on me in a television studio. During these two decades I have spent more time than I care to remember perambulating and holding forth in front of cameras. The impression I formed on that first occasion abides with me still – that the process is essentially fraudulent. I have a pathological distaste for seeing myself on television, but when, for one reason or another, I have to, I am more than ever convinced that the self I see is not me but an image, and the words I speak not mine but an echo. Away filming once, I saw scribbled on a can of film: 'Dawn for dusk.' Another time, I overheard one of the crew asking: 'Where's the plastic grass?' *Cinéma verité*?

So strong is this impression that I have come to consider the camera the most sinister of all inventions of our time. Why, when there are H-bombs, space-ships and birth pills to choose from, do I plump for the harmless necessary Brownie? Because it is so closely related to the very well-spring of human vanity and narcissism. Purporting not to be able to lie, it falsifies the more convincingly. Making fantasy truth and truth fantasy, it transforms the world into Caliban's Island, full of sounds and sweet airs, which give delight but hurt not, so that when we wake (if we ever do) we cry to sleep again. Blake, though he lived before the camera, surely foresaw its coming when he wrote:

> This Life's dim Windows of the Soul
> Distorts the Heavens from Pole to Pole,
> And leads you to believe a Lie
> When you see with, not through, the Eye.

Has there ever been a more perfect instrument for seeing with, rather than through the eye, than the camera? And what multitudes of lies it has induced belief in, as it has progressed from bleary daguerreotypes to the latest video product! That strange procession - hand-holding cameraman umbilically linked to sound-recordist, similarly laden, and bearing before him like a phallus a great gun-mike; producer and continuity girl, a large stop-watch dangling from her sweet neck, pacing in unison with the others; the whole cortège treading as delicately as caparisoned horses at a bullfight - may it not prove to be our civilization's death march?

There is undoubtedly a growing awareness that somehow or other the alleged window on the world provided by television is really a mirror, and often a distorting one at that. Feeling so, people are inclined to hit out in all directions: accusing producers, commentators and cameramen of bias, the controllers of networks of authoritarian tendencies, governments of a censorship itch, subversives of managing to insinuate themselves onto the screen for their own malign purposes, and so on. Though to Vice-President Agnew's considerable chagrin, it is undoubtedly true that successful television commentators tend to be anarchistic rather than conservative in temperament, my own conviction is that the fault lies predominantly in the camera itself rather than in any of the human agencies. Increasingly, the camera is taking over, to the point that before so very long television production may well, like everything else, be almost wholly automated, with no need for any human participation other than to maintain the machines and programme the computers.

Anyone with experience of making television programmes, of preparing and dubbing commentaries and editing film, will know what I mean. On location, in the studio and the cutting-room, the camera tends more and more to have the last word. I happened, on a tongue-in-the-hollow-tooth principle, to take a look at the second Indian programme in the luckless British Empire series, partly because the subject is one in which I have a particular interest, and partly for the egotistic reason that at one point I was asked to contribute to it, but prudently declined. As far as I could judge, the programme managed to avoid any serious mention of the main factors in the development of British India. It did, however, show a still of Sir Richard Burton, with the information that he translated the *Kama Sutra* into English. This was followed by an often-used sequence showing priaptic statuary in Hindu temples. A chance to slip in a bit of porn? An anti-Christian missionary jibe? I think not. Just that the footage happened to be to hand. In other words, the camera spoke.

Then out on location. What the camera wants is drama, something to exercise and advertise its own particular expertise. So those pictures from Vietnam of a GI setting fire to a native hut with his cigarette-lighter, or of a Viet Cong prisoner being shot out of hand. They were probably set up, but whether they were or not is as beside the point as whether Jonah really was in the belly of the whale. They were the camera's truth, and as such, valid. Likewise, one of the most famous pictures of the 1939-45 war, used a thousand times subsequently for documentary purposes, of Hitler doing a little dance of triumph when France fell before his panzers, turns out to be doctored film. The Führer's actual tread was unremarkable, but in the camera's version he will dance on through history forever.

Perhaps the most perfect manifestation of the camera's omnipotence occurred in Nigeria at the time of the Biafran War. A prisoner was to be executed by a firing squad, and the cameramen turned up in force to film the scene. Just before the command to fire was given, one of them shouted 'Cut!' His battery was dead, and needed to be replaced. Until this was done, the execution stood suspended; then, with his battery working again, he shouted 'Action!' and – bang! bang! – the prisoner fell to the ground, his death duly recorded for the delectation of millions of viewers now and hereafter.

I happened to be on telly-business in Belfast in the early days of the crisis. The place was stiff with cameras, prowling like hungry wolves. At that time, intimations of IRA activities were hard to find, and rather derisory when found. Returning some months later, how different was the scene! IRA men were two a penny, and shots of them drilling, lying in ambush, pointing automatic weapons and peering along gun-barrels as easy to come by as picture postcards of Beachy Head. I wondered then, and wonder still more now, whether any governments which permits the free, unfettered use of television will ever again be able to put down an insurrection or win a war. If the Indian population had been wired for television as we are and the Americans are, would their enthusiasm for the war against Pakistan have survived close-ups of the orphanage their Air Force bombed in Dacca, and interviews with survivors, to accompanying sound-effects? Would the Israelis have remained as whole-heartedly bellicose if, week after week, they had been fed video pictures of the sufferings of Arab refugees dispossessed of their lands and otherwise afflicted? I doubt it.

As for the words – everything has, of course, in any case to be edited down, which makes them as malleable as the pictures. Thus, it has been established that some of the interviews in the much praised programme *The Selling of the Pentagon* were fitted together in such a way as to give a completely false impression of the sense of what was said. The programme nonetheless was given awards, and continues to be held in the highest esteem. Who can wonder that Mrs Gandhi cut up rough when a French cameraman-producer, Louis Malle, went handholding through India, producing pictures of misery, destitution, cruelty and superstition. More particularly as her dangerous neighbour, China, got prestige showing of purely propaganda film on the same screens by the simple expedient of never allowing foreign camera-crews into the country except under the most rigorous control.

Likewise, the Soviet Government had every reason to congratulate itself on the television compilations shown in the West for the fiftieth anniversary of the Russian Revolution in view of the fact that, lacking documentary footage, they fell back on extracts taken from Eisenstein's films of incidents like the storming of the Winter Palace in Petrograd. *Cinema verité* again!

Christopher Ralling, a gifted BBC producer, has given expression to his concern about this no-man's-land between drama and documentary, into which makers of programmes increasingly incline to venture. More ominous and more difficult to pin down is the camera's capacity to bring happenings to pass to meet its own needs. Like the Hebrew prophets of old, ensuring that things happen in order that the prophecy may be fulfilled. Once, returning to my New York hotel, I saw a little crowd gathered; bearded men and bra-less girls holding placards, a police van near by, and a number of cops, their truncheons out, standing by. Everything set for a demo. What's happening? I asked, and was told, as though it should have been obvious, that they were waiting for the cameras. I waited, too, and saw them arrive, set up, roll; and then – Action! Placards lifted, slogans chanted, fists clenched. Pigs! Pigs! A few demonstrators arrested and pitched into the van, a few cops kicked; until – Cut! Soon, cops and demonstrators had gone, leaving the street silent and deserted.

The cameras are our ego's eyes, our rage's focus; the repository of our fraudulence. Take them into any Negro slum, any university campus, any place of conflict anywhere, and in a matter of minutes trouble stirs. Jerry Rubin, who, viewers may remember, celebrated his appearance on British television by aiming a water-pistol at David Frost and calling him a plastic man, has some relevant words on the subject. Television, he observes, creates myths bigger than reality. Whereas a demo may drag on for hours and hours, 'TV packs all the

action into two minutes – a commercial for the revolution.'
On the television screen, news is not so much reported as
created; 'an event *happens* when it goes on TV and becomes
myth.' Television, he continues, is a non-verbal instrument.
So, turn off the sound, since no one remembers any words
they hear; the mind being a technicolour movie of images,
not words. There is no such thing, he concludes, as bad cover-
age of a demo. It makes no difference what is *said*; the pictures
are the story.

Brooding upon these sagacious observations, I ask myself,
not just whether it is possible with television to win wars or
put down insurrections, but whether, ultimately, government
itself is possible. Frankly, I think not.

15

━┿═╍┿━

RUSSIA REVISITED

In 1933 there appeared in the Manchester Guardian, three articles I had written describing a visit to the Ukraine and the Caucasus, then suffering from a severe famine brought on as a direct result of Stalin's ruthless enforcement of the collectivisation of agriculture and liquidation of the so-called kulaks, or better-off peasants.

For some months previously I had been acting as the Guardian's Moscow correspondent, and hearing much talk of acute food shortages. So I decided to go and have a look at the state of affairs for myself. I knew that if I asked for official permission to undertake such a trip, either it would be refused out-of-hand, or I should be provided with a guide who would ensure that I only saw what the authorities wanted me to see, backed up by fraudulent statistics. Such were the conditions under which foreign journalists had to work, and I doubt if they are much different now.

I therefore got the Russian secretary of a fellow-correspondent, AT Cholerton, to buy me the requisite railway tickets, and set forth, making first for Rostov, and breaking my journey from time to time to look round. What I saw was unforgettably horrifying – empty villages, desperately hungry faces everywhere, neglected fields, peasants being loaded into goods-trains as alleged kulaks on their way to the labour-camps in Siberia, Solzhenitsyn's Gulag Archipelago. What I was seeing, I realised, was not just a famine, but amounted to a state of war with the peasants, and the consequent total breakdown of agriculture in some of the most fertile land in Europe.

When I got back to Moscow I wrote it all down, and sent off my three articles by diplomatic bag, obligingly made available, to ensure their safe arrival in Manchester. As I well knew, once they were published my situation in Moscow would become untenable. From being the correspondent of a paper well disposed towards the Soviet regime, and with credentials from Sidney and Beatrice Webb, my wife Kitty's uncle and aunt, who were among the most abject and uncritical of the regime's admirers – as Beatrice put it, they were icons in the USSR – I should be seen as a class enemy and anathema, and have my visa withdrawn. How many truths have been suppressed to save a visa! How many falsehoods propagated!

By the time the articles were published I had left Moscow, and no longer had any connection with the *Guardian*. The response was very much what I had expected – much criticism, and numerous accusations of my being a liar. It was not until Khrushchev's famous speech at the 20th Party Congress denouncing Stalin that I was exonerated. Khrushchev put the deaths in the famine at five million – and he surely, as an important member of the Ukrainian *Apparat*, ought to have known – and altogether gave a more drastic account than mine of the consequences of the collectivisation of agriculture. No one, in

the light of his revelations, apologised for accusing me of un-
fair and distorted reporting; the golden descriptions by Walter
Duranty, Moscow correspondent of the New York Times, of
granaries overflowing with grain, apple-cheeked dairymaids
and plump contented cows, still stood. Indeed, he received
several Pulitzer Awards for his reporting from Moscow.

In spite of a certain professional malaise resulting from my
sojourn in the USSR, I had every reason to be thankful for
it. From my point of view, it had been infinitely worthwhile,
enabling me to understand as nothing else would what the
Soviet regime was about, how it functioned and what was its
impact on neighbouring countries and the world in general.

The dream of the early Socialists, myself among them, that
the Russian Revolution would in due course bring about a
brotherly, peaceful society which had shed the lure of war
and conquest, and the exploitation of the poor by the rich,
of the weak by the powerful, was lost for ever. The Soviet
regime itself, I came to see, was about power, and little else;
the disparity between the *apparatchiks* and the workers and
peasants was, if anything, greater than between the skilled and
the unskilled, the employers and the employed in the rest of
the world.

As for bellicosity – the first priority soon became building
up the defence forces, especially the Red Army, and getting
rid of the Old Bolsheviks, the true begetters of the Russian
Revolution, by the simple expedient of inducing them by
one means or another to confess that they have been working
for foreign intelligence services and sabotaging the fulfilment
of the Five-Year Plan, and then shooting them. As a good

number of them happen to have been Jews, liquidating them touched off a reversion to traditional Russian anti-semitism.

The conundrum that continued to occupy my mind – still does for that matter – was how it came about that some of the most famous and highly esteemed intellectuals or our time, in observing and assessing the Soviet regime, should have displayed a credulity and fatuity that would be surprising in any half-wit or bemused Marxist. Thus, for instance, Bernard Shaw, expressing satisfaction that the Soviet Government balanced its budgets, and that the people of the Baltic States should have voted freely and overwhelmingly for incorporation into the USSR.

Or the venerable Dean of Canterbury, Dr Hewlett Johnson, in spite of the anti-God museums and propaganda, and the persecution of Christian believers, going on proclaiming in the pulpit that Stalin was building the Kingdom of Christ. Or Beatrice Webb, somewhat troubled by my *Guardian* articles, going to Mr Maisky, the Soviet Ambassador in London, to be put right. It was Mr Maisky, too, Beatrice Webb told me, with great satisfaction, who had been kind enough to go through the galleys of the book – Soviet Communism: A New Civilisation? – she and Sidney had written about the Soviet regime to ensure that they had made no mistakes.

Surely some future Gibbon will derive great pleasure and satisfaction from describing how the fine flower of the intelligentsia of the twentieth century were prepared to believe anything however outrageous, admire anything however cruel, excuse anything however barbarous, in order to keep intact their conviction that under the auspices of the great Stalin a new, more just, more equitable society was coming to pass.

There an office-holder on some local branch of the League of Nations Union, there a godly Quaker who once had tea with Gandhi, there scarred and worthy veterans of a hundred battles for truth and freedom, all singing the praises of the most ruthless, comprehensive and murderous dictatorship the world has yet seen.

I assumed that after the appearance of my articles on the Stalin-made famine described in them, I should always be refused a visa to enter the USSR. On the one or two occasions that I applied for one, this proved to be the case. Being thus barred, to my surprise, rather saddened me; there still remains something rather wonderful about the country itself and its people. In them, a superb stoicism, a wry, underground humour, a brotherliness in their endurance of the appalling hardships and oppression to which they are subjected. Behind the dreary, cruel proposition of Marx, one seemed to hear the ancient greeting: 'Christ is risen!'

As it happens, despite being on the black-list, I did manage to [re]visit the USSR three times. The first occasion was accidental; I happened to be in Peking, and on an impulse applied at the Soviet Embassy for a transit visa to return to London via Moscow. This was stamped into my passport without any questions being asked, and I spent several days wandering about the streets of Moscow, finding them just as before, with the same nondescript crowd drifting along them. Maybe, I reflected, the only way of ensuring that no changes take place is to have a revolution. Those who bring about the revolution know how easy it is to make one, and so stick furiously to their status quo, like a man in a cold bath who keeps quite still to avoid feeling how cold the water is.

The second occasion was accompanying Harold Macmillan on his visit to the USSR when he was Prime Minister; a guarantee had been given that no accredited journalists should be barred, and this included even me. As it turned out, it was a somewhat ribald outing, and included a visit to a collective farm near Kiev, when the Prime Minister in his speech referred to how long ago a Ukrainian princess married into the English royal family, and went on to express the hope that this amicable relationship might be renewed. The crowds that turn out for distinguished visitors in the USSR always have a top layer of Lubianka men with bulges under their arms - then the GPU, now the KGB, but the same essential personnel. I took a look at their grey, stony faces as the Prime Minister made his point about the Ukrainian princess, and observed in them, not a smile, but a tiny twitch at the corners of the mouth.

The last occasion that I visited the USSR was in connection with a series of TV programmes called *A Third Testament*, jointly commissioned by *Time* magazine and the Canadian Broadcasting Commission. I did the commentary, and two of the programmes - on Tolstoy and Dostoievsky - were filmed in the USSR. No difficulty was made about my visa, doubtless because it was applied for in Ottawa, not London.

To describe all the complications and humorous situations that arose in presenting these two great and prophetic writers in the setting of the Soviet regime would require much more space than is available here. Suffice it to say that, quoting them, thinking about them, as it were living with them, gave me very strongly the feeling that out of the suffering, the moral, spiritual and intellectual vandalism that has befallen

Russia since the Revolution, will come some great new fulfilment of the genius of the Russian people. As Solzhenitsyn
has said, there are no Marxists in the Gulag Archipelago, and
in losing freedom there, it is found.

✦

16

SOLZHENITSYN
RECONSIDERED

Ever since Solzhenitsyn's Harvard address the changed attitude of the media pundits in the West towards him has become manifest. Old media hands like myself get to know the signs - the casual innuendo, the throwaway line ('not the liberal we would like him to be'), the tone more in sorrow than in anger, the barking in unison as the consensus pack moves collectively towards the kill. It was in the Harvard address that he deviated most drastically from the basic liberal orthodoxy that freedom consists in being allowed and provided with the means to do whatever anyone has a mind to, and that a free society is one in which this is possible and the means readily available, the supreme example of such a society being, of course, the United States.

What magnified his offence from the consensus point of view, making it quite intolerable, was that, on his own admission, Solzhenitsyn derived his view of freedom from the New Testament rather than from such impeccable sources as the American Declaration of Independence and the judgments of the US Supreme Court, in effect repeating to his Harvard audience what he had already written in his 'Letter to the Soviet leaders: 'I myself see Christianity today as the only living spiritual force capable of undertaking the spiritual healing of Russia.'

In his Gulag books Solzhenitsyn established once and for all the role and extent of forced labour camps as an instrument of terrorism in the USSR. Thenceforth, thanks to him, apologists for the Soviet regime will have to take due account of the Gulag Archipelago rather than, as heretofore, seeking to deny its existence, or, like the ineffable Eleanor Roosevelt, dishing it up as part of as essentially humane penal system. Then, in his autobiographical work, *The Oak and the Calf*, he deals with the pains and penalties of a writer in the USSR, describing his own experiences as a dissident writer between his release from the labour camps and his expulsion abroad in 1974.

In a sense, of course, all serious writers are in some degree dissidents; but whereas in the so-called free world their concern is to earn a living in a society in which porn is a mighty industry and literature a campus waste-product, in the USSR conformity with the party line is obligatory, and to deviate from it in word or even in thought can involve, not just penury and obscurity, but a one-way ticket to the Gulag Archipelago as well. As a sometime political prisoner, or, in Soviet slang, a Zek, Solzhenitsyn was not allowed to come to Moscow. So, on his release, he worked as a teacher of mathematics in the provinces, devoting all his spare time and energies to writing.

In ordinary circumstances the procedure would have been to submit his work to some local or national publication or publishing setup. In Solzhenitsyn's case this was precluded because the subject of his writings has been precisely the terrorism and mental chicanery whereby a Marxist oligarchy has ruthlessly imposed its will and ideology on a subservient population. Being a Zek himself, Solzhenitsyn felt a duty to the others he had left behind in the Gulag Archipelago to speak up for them, telling his fellow countrymen and the world about their suffering and privations and the monstrous injustice of their treatment. In all that he has written and spoken and done he has been true to this duty. And, let it be remembered, he could perfectly well have settled, as, for instance, Maxim Gorky did, for being a distinguished Soviet author, free to travel abroad, well provided with foreign currency, and honoured at home as well as abroad. All that would be required of him would be to keep off a few sensitive themes, but this was just what he was in no circumstances prepared to do. In the early thirties, as I well remember, on important occasions Gorky used to be brought on to the platform along with Stalin and the Politburo, looking for all the world like a performing seal - a role that would never have suited Solzhenitsyn even though Gorky's reward was a commodious villa in Italy and a visa to come and go there.

Solzhenitsyn has the honesty to admit that his self-imposed duty has proved arduous and often frustrating. When he completed the first draft of *The Oak and the Calf* in the spring of 1967 he entertained a hope that he might be released from the agonizing role he had chosen for himself of being the Zeks' champion. Six years later when he prepared the text for publication he asked himself more urgently than ever when the din of battle would cease for him. 'If only,' he writes, 'I could go away from it all, go away many years to the back of beyond with nothing but fields and open skies and woods and horses in sight, and nothing to do but write my novel at my own pace.' Now, in enforced exile, he has the additional anguish of observing how, in the West, where the means to be free still exist, people have wearied of freedom, finding it an intolerable burden, and are all unconsciously sleep-walking into the very servitude Solzhenitsyn has so valiantly and faithfully resisted and denounced.

In the circumstances in which he was placed on his release from the labour camps he had no choice but to hide away his writings as he completed them, in the expectation that they would one day be published and fulfil their purpose. In every moment away from his teaching, he tells us, he wrote and wrote, diligently, day after day, and sometimes night after night. When, as a veteran free-lance practitioner, I think of the difficulty of producing commissioned copy to meet a deadline, I marvel at the books he produced in this manner, so brilliantly, so conscientiously, and so nobly disinterested in their purpose. Take the case of the Gulag books, very dear to his heart, and not just a literary feat of the highest order, but, as well, an integral part of the history of our time, and for that reason alone ever memorable. They were no mere exercise in writing; he had to collect in the greatest secrecy the testimonies on which the books are based, at the same time scrupulously protecting his sources in the knowledge that the consequences for them would be ruinous if it came out that they had provided him with information. Nonetheless, the books were completed while he was still living in the USSR; and in due course a copy of the manuscript was sent abroad, so that whatever might happen to him, the peoples of the West would know what the Gulag Archipelago was like and what it signified to Russians and others forcibly absorbed into the Soviet sphere of influence.

In his career as an undercover writer Solzhenitsyn was greatly beholden to Samizdat, the clandestine publishing system established in the USSR; and steadily growing in output and influence. Now it has spread through the whole country, and its productions are printed, not hand-written or cyclostyled as in the early days. All Solzhenitsyn's forbidden works have been circulated by Samizdat, and have reached tens of thousands of readers despite the KGB's efforts to stop it. With one or two notable exceptions – latterly none – it can be taken for granted that whatever serious literature is being produced by the so-gifted Russian people bears the Samizdat imprint. Some notion of the gap between what Samizdat publishes and the officially produced volumes displayed in the bookshops, may be deduced from the recent award of the Lenin Prize for Literature to Brezhnev, whose flat-footed sentences in his speeches and addresses can scarcely be considered prize worthy. If Western publishers wanted to retaliate for the fiasco of their efforts to hold a bookfair in Moscow, a good idea would be to mount a Samizdat exhibition in London or New York and ask Solzhenitsyn to open it. I can't, however, see them doing this.

The big break came for Solzhenitsyn when none other than Nikita Khrushchev, while still the head man in the Kremlin, praised his book, *One Day in the Life of Ivan Denisovich*, about life in the labour camps, and authorized its publication in the USSR. How exactly this came about remains obscure, and anyway shortly afterwards Khrushchev reverted to the worst kind of Stalinist censorship. Nonetheless, the book was duly published and widely acclaimed, so that Solzhenitsyn became a celebrity at home and abroad. Also – which was more important for him – he came into contact with *Novy Mir*, the leading literary magazine in the USSR, and its editor, Tvardovsky. Solzhenitsyn's account of this truly remarkable man, and of the relationship between them, with all its ups and downs, makes fascinating reading.

Tvardovsky was torn between joy in his own literary talent and genuine appreciation of literature and of Solzhenitsyn's genius, and his satisfaction at finding himself a member of the top Soviet elite, with all the privileges that went therewith, including a *dacha* in a restricted area – an inner conflict that led him, like so many of his fellow countrymen, to resort increasingly to vodka. The affection between the two men survived all hazards, and when, as a result of a stroke, Tvardovsky became helpless and incoherent, Solzhenitsyn sat patiently and lovingly at his bedside. At his funeral he mourned his passing, both for Russia's sake, and on his own account. In a particularly venomous attack on Solzhenitsyn in *Harper's* magazine, George Feifer alleges that in his account of his transactions with *Novy Mir* and Tvardovsky, Solzhenitsyn has vilified both. What Solzhenitsyn does show – and I am sure justly – is that *Novy Mir*, despite its good record in Soviet terms, has no choice when it comes to the crunch but to obey its political masters. Likewise Tvardovsky, despite the essential nobility of his character.

Even now, in retrospect, it is hard to make any sense of the vacillations of Soviet policy in dealing with Solzhenitsyn.

After the fame he acquired from the publication of *One Day in the Life of Ivan Denisovich* he soon found himself once again being trailed by the KGB, as well as excluded from *Novy Mir* and expelled from the Writer's Union, an organisation wholly controlled by the authorities. Some years ago I had a glimpse of its members when I was standing in front of its headquarters – located in the house Tolstoy chose as the model for the Rostov residence in *War and Peace* – beside a huge statue of Tolstoy, and holding forth about him for a TV programme. While I was speaking members were coming and going, and may well have been voting on the infamous motion to expel Solzhenitsyn from the Union, which would account for the hangdog air they all seemed to have.

As the struggle to silence Solzhenitsyn went on, he fought back single-handedly, and managed to hold his own for a time, until his expulsion abroad – which he half dreaded and half wanted – settled matters. At one point it became known that a certain Victor Louis had taken a copy of Solzhenitsyn's *Cancer Ward* to the West to dispose of it on behalf of the KGB, having previously performed a similar service for the KGB with a manuscript by Stalin's daughter Alliluyeva. This Victor Louis is altogether an odd figure; his real name it seems, is Vitaly Levin, and besides being a legman for the KGB, he has acted as Moscow correspondent for the London *Evening News* – a combination of duties which supports the saying that, journalistically speaking, a dateline, like ripeness, is all.

Running through everything Solzhenitsyn has written about his struggle to stand up to 'them', the present masters and manipulators of the Russian people, there is the assumption of his Christian faith. He neither expounds nor stresses it, but the reader is conscious of it all the time – acquired in the Gulag Archipelago, where, being totally deprived of freedom in earthly terms, he came to understand what constituted true freedom, the glorious liberty of the children of God about which the Apostle Paul speaks so eloquently. In the second Gulag book, in the wonderful chapter called 'The Ascent', he even refers thankfully to his time in the labour camps as having brought him this illumination, and I truly believe that he would have found it more congenial to resume his old Zek existence rather than to watch, as he has had to do in his compulsory exile, the continuing surrender to 'them' of whatever power, authority, and influence still pertains to what we go on calling Western civilization.

Now with the consensus pack after him, and with his Western readers, requiring variety, to sustain their interest, and the crazed expectations of an illusory kingdom of heaven on earth, such as he cannot possibly provide, his immediate worldly prospects must be considered uncertain. Yet there is no sign of his own courage and determination faltering. 'In moments of weakness and distress,' he writes, 'it is good to tread closely in ˙ God's footsteps.' How amazed and incredulous I should have been as a young journalist in Moscow in the early thirties, given to pottering about the anti-God museums which then proliferated in the USSR, if someone had told me that half a century later one of the very finest products of the regime would be writing in this strain:

'Where would I be in a few days time – in jail or happily working at my novel? God alone knows. I prayed. I could have enjoyed myself so much, breathing the fresh air, resting, stretching my cramped limbs, but my duty to the dead permitted no such self-indulgence. They are dead. You are alive. Do your duty. The world must know *all about it*'.

Well, thanks largely to Solzhenitsyn, the world now does know all about it, but his battle with 'them' goes on. It is one man against the Kremlin, which might seem hopeless odds, but when that one man is Solzhenitsyn against all the odds he must win, since, as he concludes in his splendid Nobel Prize lecture: '*One word of truth outweighs the world*.' It is on this 'seemingly fantastic violation of the law of the conservation of mass and energy' that he has based all the activities on behalf of his old Zek comrades he so movingly describes in *The Oak and the Calf.* In the course of describing them he tells more about himself than has been revealed in his other writings, and more about the Soviet regime, its inner reality, than any other book I know of in the vast literature dealing with the October Revolution and its consequences.

17

THE LAW OF LOVE AND THE
LAW OF VIOLENCE

*T*he *Law of Love* and *The Law of Violence* consists of almost
the last words Tolstoy wrote. Everything Tolstoy wrote is
precious, but I found this final statement of the truth about
life as he had come to understand it particularly beautiful and
moving. 'That is what I have wanted to say to you, my brothers. Before I died.' So he concludes, giving one a vivid sense
of the old man, pen in hand and bent over the paper, his forehead wrinkled into a look of puzzlement very characteristic
of him, as though he were perpetually wondering how others
could fail to see what was to him so clear - that the law of
love explained all mysteries and invalidated all other laws.

His last theme is the one to whose presentation and exposition he devoted so much of his time and genius - the
everlasting confrontation between love and violence, between
the imagination and the will, between Christ and Caesar.
Freedom from servitude, he was always insisting, cannot be
achieved through collective effort, through the capture or
exercise of power in order to change the external forms of
authority, but only through the liberation of men's souls from

the evil that is harboured within them. No more can human happiness be advanced through the creation and distribution of wealth:

'Each step we make today towards material progress not only does not advance us towards the general well-being, but shows us, on the contrary, that all these technical improvements only increase our miseries. One can imagine other machines, submarine, subterranean and aerial, for transporting men with the rapidity of lightning; one could multiply to infinity the means of propagating human speech and thought, but it would remain no less the case that these travellers, so comfortably and rapidly transported, are neither willing nor able to commit anything but evil, and the thoughts and words they pour forth would only incite men to further harm. As to the beautifully perfected armaments of destruction, which, while diminishing the risk of those who employ them, make carnage easier, they only give further proof of the impossibility of persevering in the direction we are going.'

A prophetic utterance! Before a decade had passed a revolution was to take place in his own country, Russia, in the name of freedom and brotherliness, resulting in a regime of unexampled brutality and servitude. Before half a century had passed two world wars, using and developing all technological possibilities, would destroy millions of lives, degrade millions more, and leave behind a cultural and spiritual wasteland. Before the century was out the dedication to power and wealth as the essential instruments of justice and progress, and to money and sensual indulgence as the essential means to happiness, was to be complete, with the clergy well to the fore in underwriting Caesar's kingdom in the name of Christ.

If Tolstoy still occasionally casts an eye in our direction, it will surely be considered permissible, even in celestial company, for him to summon up one of his old ironical smiles at our present discomfiture, recalling, maybe, another of his last sayings: 'He who is guided by self-interest alone cannot do otherwise than deceive or be deceived.'

It is easy to see why Tolstoy equally enraged the authorities, the revolutionaries and the Church. The authorities because he held up to ridicule and scorn the notion of authority as such, based, as it must be whatever its form, on the wickedness of violence and the falsity of law. The revolutionaries because he insisted that merely overturning one regime by violence only led to another likewise based on violence. The Church because he used the words of the New Testament to rebuke and denounce the ostensible spokesmen of Christ on earth. His writings were censored and sometimes suppressed; the advocates of change, whether violent or constitutional, derived no comfort from his words; ecclesiastics pursued him with the malignancy reserved for those who love truth.

Yet everyone listened to him. That is the extraordinary thing. The voice of this inspired moujik, this strange sensualist-saint, this sublime genius whose words had, and have, a magical glow and force, was heard everywhere. What he had to say does not, in terms of practical human behaviour, make sense. Though he often quotes Pascal, he lacked his inspired clarity of thought. The essential dilemma with which he deals in *the Law of Love and the Law of Violence* remains unresolved. How can we live peacefully and brotherly together in this world without resort to violence, just on a basis of Christ's gospel of love. Not requiring or enforcing laws; not meeting violence with violence, leaving even a Hitler or a Stalin to have his way; meekly accepting the yoke of whichever fraud or gangster or buffoon happens to seize power, in the expectation that 'as soon as men understand that their participation in violence is incompatible with the Christianity they profess, as soon as they refuse to serve as soldiers, tax collectors, judges, jury, and police agents, the violence from which the whole world suffers will disappear forthwith.'

Of course it hasn't disappeared and I suppose never will. Tolstoy writes somewhere about a peasant belief that a green stick had been buried in the earth and would one day be found, and then all our troubles would come to an end. I think he half believed it himself, and was always on the look out for the green stick, until at last he grew tired of looking. Never mind. The fact that a man like Tolstoy could exist amounts in itself to a green stick. It is true that today his hopes seem more remote even than when he entertained them. Yet underlying the disappointed hopes was his faith in a single infallible guide, a 'Universal Spirit that lives in men as a whole, and in each one of us . . . that commands the tree to grow towards the sun, the flower to throw off its seed in autumn, and us to reach out towards God and by so doing become united to each other.' Such was his last word, delivered to us, his brothers, who come after him.

18

LETTERS TO KITTY

November 4, 1962

Arizona

My own sweet Darling, I've thought about you so much during these weeks, practically all the time, and always lovingly; despite the anguish over Val, in a glowing sort of way. Everything seems clearer to me then it's ever been before. In helping Val in some weird way you help me. I don't quite understand how this happens. It's quite plain what we've got to do about Val – love her, help her, look after her in all circumstances. No life, I'm certain, can be wasted, and the worth of a life cannot be estimated in human terms.

November 10, 1962

San Francisco

I long to hear how Val is coming along. One of the girls from the college I spoke at last night came to interview me, and mentioned that she'd been in psychiatric wards and institutions for six years. She seemed very sweet and self-possessed, and yet she said each day she didn't go back was a day gained.

This kind of thing is going on all the time here. I asked her if the psychiatrists had helped her, and she said they were for the most part quite at sea, and that she'd been discharged as incurable. The impression she made on me was of being so much saner than most Americans. A day or so ago I scribbled down;

'I seem unaccountably, to be having a love affair with all life. Every time my mind relaxes a sense of ecstasy sweeps over me such as I have rarely, if ever, before experienced. This despite the fact that my days are rather absurdly spent wandering about America, and delivering some dog-eared jokes and observations to largely uncomprehending audiences.'

November 19, 1962

Pennsylvania

I hope so much my darling Val is going on getting better, and that it's not been too much of a strain for you. The answer for us all, V included, is very simple. We're all in the same boat, and the only thing to do is to gamble everything on this very simple answer, fighting off the dark enemies when they assail one, which they ceaselessly do and ever will. Only every time one drives them off they're feebler in the next assault and one's stronger, with an extraordinary happiness, even ecstasy welling up inside one.

December 3, 1962

New York

I was so happy to find a letter from you awaiting me here. I spent yesterday (Sunday) walking about Chicago. I must have walked at least ten miles. It's the only thing I can find to do in

this country where I don't want anything and am on my own
– to abnormal conditions which makes one a sort of outcast.
They don't like you to sit alone in restaurants or to walk alone
in streets. It's unseemly, if not downright sinister.

Last week at the airport of Dayton, Ohio, it was a lovely day
and I decided to go for a stroll through a maize field while
waiting for my plane. I'd scarcely got going when a police car
came after me, it wasn't allowed, and I had to go back in the
car. It was the first time, as I told the copper, that I'd actually
been arrested for walking, though I was well aware it was
considered an eccentricity bordering on insanity. My darling,
I only want to be with you, and have no other wish in this
world.

April 30, 1964

New Delhi

The journey was uneventful, except that Nehru's sister was
aboard, and met at each stopping place by little bands of
sycophantic countrymen. It's very hot, but dry and bearable.
Tomorrow we go to Simla. The programme is, I can see, going to be even more difficult then I'd thought, and Kevin and
I are still floundering about with ideas rather then concrete
notions.

May 4, 1964

Simla

It was a great relief to get up in the mountains. Down below
it's really appallingly hot. We have to return there in a week's
time. This morning reading Leonard Woolf's description of

the Downs and Rodmell I felt an almost unbearable longing to be back with you in Robertsbridge. Woolf describes
rather movingly, and not in the least dramatically, how poor
Virginia used to go bonkers from time to time. These break-
downs seem to follow an invariable course. In their case the
head-shrinkers advised that she shouldn't have children because the nervous strain would be too much. As usual the
diametrically wrong advice, I should have thought.

May 10, 1964

Delhi

I was so overjoyed to get your telegram and then letter. For
some reason I'd got into a state of panic about you, and was
homesick. There's something so bizarre about this expedition
that I keep on wondering why I should be here and what
I'm supposed to be doing. So far everything that could go
wrong has. The camera crew were held up two days en route,
and now the chief cameraman is sick. Things keep breaking (including, today, the weather), and every appointment
is at the wrong time in the wrong place. It's a bit like all the
Tutankamen disasters. Perhaps one isn't meant to delve into
one's life on the telly; sacrilegious or something. You'll have
gathered from Jean that the ES job has come to an end. I'm
very relieved. Now I want to get out of these regular journalistic assignments and concentrate on other writing. The big,
indeed the only, dividend in what I'm doing now is the great
impetus it's given to thoughts about my Autobiog.

May 22, 1964

Calcutta

Today thank God we leave Calcutta for Alwaye, and the last lap of the programme. It's been pretty arduous but I feel that the worst is over. All the while I keep saying over to myself what the old beggar in Roquebrune said when his dog died: 'Le Chagrin ne sert a rien.' However, Le Chagrin occasionally boils up, I regret to say.

October 15, 1964

Chicago

If only I were with you! The moment you can get away make for Toronto, and then we can join up wherever I happen to be. If you can't get away I shall try and abbreviate my stay and leave on November 20ᵗʰ or thereabouts. I'd leave before, tomorrow, if I could; but I can't with this camera crew here and these lecture engagements. I only want to be with you.

October 25, 1964

New York

I got two letters today, to great relief and delight. They brought good news – that V was better, that you'd weathered the storm. No one but you would have. All my love, all my hopes, all my prayers, all my everything are with you all the time, but you've had to tackle this terrible experience of V out of her mind on your own. I should so love it if you could get away for a bit. How about going to Toronto early in November, and then joining me in New York on the 8ᵗʰ for a few days; then back to Toronto and with me again on the

20th. It would be so wonderful as it now appears I shall now have to be over here till Dec 6th when I do a Paar programme. Your sweet company would break up the exile. How about that? Only you can decide, of course; but if it's at all possible, for your own sake as well as mine, you should come.

October 30, 1964

California

How marvellous that I shall probably be seeing you soon in New York. I'm leaving Los Angeles today with relief. It's not a nice place. How I long and long and long to be with you. The only thing for me has been work, and I've done a lot and earned a fair amount of dough. But it's not the work I want to be doing; at least not altogether. Never mind, I feel, terrifically ready for my real work, which is yet to be done, and am looking forward more then I can say to being in Roquebrune with you and V, and going for those lovely walks.

April 18, 1967

Nunraw

My Own Sweet Darling, how delighted I was to get your letter today. I really miss you more and more, and hate every day you're not with me. Although all here are as nice as they could be I'm rather longing for the whole thing to be over. Towards the end of next week I'll be back in Robertsbridge. I should think it would probably be Friday, or even Saturday, but I'll telephone nearer the time.

On Friday the 5th I find I took on an Any Questions programme in Gloucester, and on Sunday the 7th I have to speak

in the University Church at Cambridge. Then all my com-
mitments are over, and I'm going to stay in Robertsbridge
without stirring till we go to the Holy Land in September.
The country round here is marvellous in a way, but swept by
a chill wind most of the time. As for the Abbey itself – I love
the monks, but find them somehow tragic. What they're doing is heroic, but it's like a cavalry charge against an armoured
division; they sing their offices very sweetly, but the sound
is thin. They've built their fine new Abbey, but I think they
wonder – as I do – whether they'll ever move into it. The
most cheerful and robust among them are the Irish peasants.
One of these – Brother Oliver – told me yesterday how he'd
heard a tinker woman in Ireland say: 'When you've lost your
flower you must hawk your bran.' What a splendid sentence!

Aug 2, 1967

Jerusalem

We've made a start, and have already met Dr Tester of Nazareth, who turns out to be a delightful man. I'll be driving to
Tel Aviv with him to meet you and the Frazers on your arrival. On Tuesday I'm going to Nazareth to see the flat. This
hotel is delightful; in what was the Arab part of the town, and
I shall hope to spend a night or so with you here during your
stay. Chris and I have already started looking around; please
have a read of the NT before you come so as to get some
ideas. Study the life of Christ as though it were a biog. that
you were going to write, as you did B's. This could be invalu-
able to us. The weather is pleasant, but fairly hot; just about
like Egypt. No need for warm clothes, but one sweater for the
evenings if one sits outside.

Sep 4, 1967

Jerusalem

My Darling, As I hear the posts are bad I'm taking advantage of a man here going to London to send this. The Christian shrines are quite horrible; so ugly and fraudulent. Why bother to set up anti-God museums when there's the Church of the Holy Sepulchre?

So far the programme's a bit stagnant, but I'm hoping to see things more clearly after visiting the Nazareth people. We go there tomorrow. I miss you horribly, and our quiet life at Robertsbridge which I love so much - the reading, the music etc etc. Just now I'm sorry I ever took this on, but no doubt that mood will change. I'll telephone you anyway before you leave, so any last-minute thoughts can be exchanged then.

Oct 9, 1967

Jerusalem

The time passes quickly now, and I'll be back before we know where we are. As plans are at present we finish the Life of Christ film round about the 28th and then Ben Gurion for three or four days. I'd expect to be back on the 3rd or fourth. There's a new man coming out to direct the BG programme and I'm going to ask him to bring out a warm jacket - the new tweed - as it's getting very fresh in Jerusalem. He'll get in touch with you about it. The film seems to be going well, but there are the usual camera-crew angsts; nothing serious. I'm going down to BG's kibutz to see him tomorrow; then we'll film round about in the weird desert country you saw. After that to Nazareth again, and then we'll be getting towards the end. I expect you've got your book now in all its newness; I long to see it. Graham was here for some days, and in Galilee; rather woebegone, and fond as I am of him I was rather glad when he went. He saddened me so, whereas at the Nazareth hospital they always cheer me up to the skies; especially the German Mother - what an enchanting woman!

March 11, 1968

New York

Here I am with all the lecturing done on the last lap, and wishing more than ever that I was back in Robertsbridge with you. This place is very weird just now, with a curfew and troops still patrolling the streets at night. Now I have to switch my mind and grapple with this subject of news-gathering - the pursuit of a fantasy; very difficult on the telly. On my long air journey yesterday I read St Augustine, and underlined this: 'I no longer wished for a better world, because I was thinking of the whole of creation, and in the light of this clearer discernment I had come to see that though the higher things are better than the lower, the sum of all creation is better than the higher things alone.' Good, don't you think?

April 30, 1968

Washington

I got your dear letter yesterday, and it made me more than ever long to be back in Robertsbridge with you. I keep on thinking of my darling Valentine; we've had such unspeakable good fortune apart from this one sorrow. Curiously enough this time I don't feel any kind of savage grief; I just know that pain and suffering are an essential part of the experience of living, and that this is our pain and suffering. I'm happy to say that I love Val more than ever and that I think of her as a particularly exquisite person. Why the poor darling should be called on to suffer these descents into the pit I don't know, but I do know what is expected of us, and this we'll accord her in the fullest possible measure to the day of our deaths. Anyway, my sweet darling, of all my good fortune the greatest was you, and I think of you at this moment with inexpressible gratitude and inexpressible love. This prayer of St Augustine's appealed to me: 'Let me offer you in sacrifice the service of my thoughts and my tongue, but first give me what I may offer you.'

April 5, 1969

India

I loved getting your letter and hearing about Valentine. What you say is so true; she has the immense spiritual strength of someone who has fallen into the Slough and then pulled herself out. I had a letter from her full of plans and happiness; quite different from any I'd ever had before. It gives me a feeling of contentment so overwhelming that I feel that if I were to die I should scarcely notice. I've just got back to Delhi from Gandhi's Ashram in Ahmedabad where we recorded a long conversation with his grand-daughter; a jaunty, bouncy little creature rather like an Indian Thelma Cazalet. The Gandhi legend doesn't really bear examination as now purveyed, but I'm doing my best with it out of respect for the basic principles involved. It's hard going; there's throughout an undertow of sententiousness which I find very unpalatable.

As usual, one turns for comfort to comedy; he had a strong sense of the absurd – rather like Picasso's. In fact I think he and Picasso in some weird way were rather alike; even in appearance for that matter. The screw is always being turned a little harder, I find, and on Tuesday I have to open an exhibition of cartoons about Gandhi, many of them from *Punch*. This is something – as Hughie would have said – which Dante hadn't thought of. Immediately after we go to Calcutta to deal with Mother Teresa, which I'm looking forward to. She's got a children's home here which we filmed, and I found it very touching. Young Indian nuns with these kids picked up from the streets, some of them batty; one little girl quite off her head, but with a winning smile which never deserted her. I'm ticking off the days as usual to when I get back to Robertsbridge and you; I only feel about a quarter alive when I'm away from you. So I can't tell you how inexpressibly dear to me you are; you have to know.

Love

Malcolm

19

THE HOLY LAND

In the general upheaval caused by the recent Arab-Israeli fighting, one consequence, not in itself world-shattering, perhaps, but still highly significant, is that the Christian holy places are now for the first time in the history of Christendom in Jewish hands. An Israeli soldier armed with a sub-machine gun is on guard at the entrance to the Church of the Holy Sepulchre which contains Christ's alleged tomb; another stands outside the Church of the Nativity in Bethlehem beneath which is Christ's alleged birthplace. Coinciding with the exoneration of the Jews by the Papacy of responsibility for the Crucifixion, they have become custodians of Christianity's most sacred shrines and relics, and at the same time – as I discovered, particularly, among professors at the Hebrew University, not to mention Mr Ben Gurion – obsessively interested in Christian theology and the person of Christ. It is as though the accumulated suppressed curiosity of two thousand years about one who is, after all, on any showing the most famous Jew of all, had at last found an outlet.

Reflecting on the strange turn of fate which has brought about this state of affairs, it occurred to me that a conversation on the subject between Ciaphas, Pilate and Herod – supposing they all three find themselves within hailing distance of one another – would be most interesting. In exploring the theme, I decided, they would surely cast an eye in the direction of the so-called Wailing Wall – all that remains of the magnificent Temple of their time – where, also under Israeli military supervision, bearded Rabbis in fur hats and shawls and long black flapping coats gather in strength to address their prayers and lamentations to Jehovah. It was a scene that had a powerful attraction for me; wailing, as a response to human life, increasingly seems to me highly appropriate. I loved the Rabbis' faces, so serene, so remote from the hateful twentieth century, so utterly unlike a with-it clergyman trying to popularise the Gospels among the young by topping them up with pop music and four-letter words.

Being in Israel for the purpose of participating as commentator in the making of three half-hour films on the story of Christ for BBC Television, I had every reason to interest myself more in the holy places and even the Wall than in the Jordan West Bank or the Syrian Heights or any of the other ticklish situations resulting from the war. As a matter of fact it was for me personally a new and agreeable experience to be in a place where news was emanating without having any occasion to take a professional interest in it – like, if I may make the comparison without indecorum, Maupassant's Maison Tellier off duty for a pious occasion.

What a relief to be able to reply, when asked whether I'd care to meet, say, the Mayor of Jerusalem to discuss with him the problems which had arisen in taking over the Arab part of the city, that as it happened on this particular occasion I was exclusively concerned with events twenty centuries before, and with persons long since dead – with one possible exception, and there not even the efficient and resourceful Press Department of the Israeli Foreign Office could hope to be of any help. (No reflection, by the way, on His Worship, who is by all accounts a most capable and estimable man.)

Actually, of course, one was involved, willy-nilly, in the Israeli situation. Twenty centuries ago or now makes very little difference where news is concerned; history is only news strategically, rather than tactically, slanted. As in chess, though the games seem at the time to be all different, the moves are invariable from generation to generation. It is one of the illusions of an age of scientific credulity like ours that changes of unique significance are taking place, and we like our prophets – a Marshall McLuhan, and Edmund Leach – to tell us so, with a wave of the hand abolishing our social institutions and values, and, metaphorically speaking, fitting us out with new ones; or, alternatively, in the manner of a Bertrand Russell, apocalyptically pronouncing the end of the whole human story. In either case, our sense of being unique is bolstered up, whether as the privileged initiators of a brave new world, or as the positively last denizens of a doomed old one.

To go and film by the River Jordan (how delectable a river, by the way, and so tiny to be so famous!) we required a military permit procured from the Israeli Military Governor in Jericho. It was the same old set-up, so familiar in the 1939-45 or any other war – the requisitioned house with its battered furniture, the ricketty typewriter, the cyclostyled forms, the self-important officer condescendingly granting or withholding favours according to his mood, the cigarette smoke, the army blanket covering a trestle table, even down to the frowsty ATS, secretary-vivandieres who also serve.

It seems that military occupations are invariable whenever and wherever they take place; I bet the Disciples had to apply at just such an office to get the Roman countersign on their passes to go from Caperneum to Jerusalem. The officer at Jericho who dealt with us failed to kindle at the notion that our purpose in wanting to go to a restricted area was solely concerned with Christ's baptism. Didn't all that happen a very long time ago? he seemed to be saying. And anyway, why bring it up now, when there were so many more serious matters afoot – like exchanging shots across the Jordan, and ensuring that Arabs take the Allenby Bridge to leave Israel rather than for coming in. In the end, rather grudgingly, he gave us our pass and a patronising nod; by waving it we managed to pass various control-points and a couple of tanks, and found ourselves at last on the river bank, at the traditional place of baptism.

Victory brings out the worst in everyone, and this applies to the Jews no less than to others. Yet somehow in their case it is more shocking. Is this because we expect more of the Jews than of others in the way of resisting the baser impulses? Or – as they think – because we're so used to seeing them at the receiving end of persecution that we can't bear them in the role of victors? Whatever the reason, I was quite abnormally horrified to see in Jerusalem two Arabs, one of them very youthful, being arrested, beaten up, and then, with black bags over their heads, driven away at top speed in a jeep. I wanted to rush after them, shouting impotently: 'It's like Berlin; you shouldn't be doing this!'

Another disagreeable incident happened when we were filming by the Lake of Galilee: We had with us five Arabs from Nazareth who were to walk in front of our camera. A middle-aged Israeli in a flowered shirt, obviously on holiday with his family, spotted them, and came across self-important-ly to tell us that they were not entitled to be in that area. His malignancy – somehow accentuated by the flowered shirt and sun-baked face with its gleaming spectacles – was horrible. Of course, in the circumstances, it is all perfectly understandable. Yet how sad, I reflected, if the most gifted race the world has known should succeed in transforming itself into a second-class, and perhaps second-rate, Middle-Eastern nation!

The great function of the Jews has surely been to provide an incomparable running parody of the ways of power. This is what the Hebrew prophets were about, and all those incom-parably brilliant Jewish clowns and cartoonists; as also – at the sublimest level – the hero of our film. When He said that His kingdom was not of this world, all earthly kingdoms were abolished for ever. Now the Jews have a kingdom – Israel – where they have no recourse but to parody themselves. Were the Israelis, perhaps, I wondered, the very last Sahibs? Was Israel the positively last version of the White Man's Burden?

The Christian shrines themselves, and the extensive sou-venir and relic trade which has grown up around them, provided another inescapable contact with present-day Israel. What about a crown of thorns, locally manufactured, mod-estly priced? Or a flask of Jordan water – the real stuff? Or a cross made of wood from the Mount Olives? As there were few foreign tourists because of the war, we were the target of all the vendors, who gathered round us, desperately waving and rattling their rosaries, crucifixes and other impediments. Local tourists – charabanc-loads of Israelis from Tel Aviv and Haifa – came pouring into what had been Jordan, and traipsed listlessly through the Christian shrines, churches and monasteries. Some of the monks found the scanty attire of the Israeli girls disturbing; one, a little man with one eye, in a Greek Orthodox monastery high above the desert, and seemingly hewn out of rock, told me with the utmost satisfaction of how two of these girls had fallen down a gorge and been killed.

The most famous of the shrines, the Church of the Holy Sepulchre, remains propped up with scaffolding, the necessity thus to prop it up, as a delightful French Dominican explained to me, being the only point of agreement the various sects and denominations who control the church have ever been able to find. Agreement on the next step eludes them. On the Sunday that I went, two masses – a Coptic and a Greek Orthodox – were in progress in adjoining chapels, with the celebrants literally yelling against one another. It seemed all too true an image of the present plight of Christendom.

Bethlehem, from my point of view, was little better. We went there early in the day, and I sat by myself in the cave underneath the Church of the Nativity where Christ is supposed to have been born. The actual spot is marked with a silver star, and nearby is a hollowed out stone, allegedly the manger. Overhead are numerous silver and bronze lamps, and the stone walls are covered with silk and damask, now mostly threadbare.

Seated there in the half-light, a fit of melancholy seized me; the essential point of Christ's birth, as I see it, is that it

happened in the humblest and poorest circumstances conceivable. He, who was to be worshipped through twenty
centuries by the most ardent spirits and perceptive minds of
a great civilisation, was born more obscurely than probably
anyone else that day in the whole world. What a stupendous
moment in history - when for the first time men were to see
their god, not in terms of wealth or power or pulchritude,
but of penury, weakness and obscurity. I loved the bare stone
of the cave's walls, and resented the coloured hangings which
hid it, thereby hiding the true significance of Christ's birth,
and of what His life and death were to fulfil. Truly we humans
have an astonishing faculty for thus snatching fantasy from
the jaws of truth. It is not just that history is distorted or falsified; it becomes its own opposite. From the first Christmas to
Christmas 1967, from Golgotha to the crowning of a Pope,
from St Paul to the Bishop of Woolwich, from Bethlehem to
Regent Street - such is history's gamut, which we must run.

It was a great relief to get to Galilee, where I forgot the
shrines and suddenly felt happy. The Lake, the hills, even the
ruins of Tiberias and Caperneum - it was all somehow perfect, uncontaminated, miraculous. One realised that in some
mysterious way only in this land could Christ's mission have
been undertaken and fulfilled; nowhere else. Its earth and its
contours, its very texture and vegetation, were a book in which
the Christian story was written, and where it could always be
read. In that sense, despite everything, it *was* truly a Holy Land.

We followed out the story as best we might - climbing up
the Mount of Beatitudes to listen to that stupendous sermon;
going out into the desert to encounter the devil and with
his three temptations - to turn stones into bread and thus

augment the Gross National Product, to fly to the moon and thus impress the unbelieving, and to take over the kingdoms of the earth to ensure the everlasting reign in them of life, liberty and the pursuit of happiness.

We saw the fishermen lay down their nets and go running after a voice which called them; we heard the poor lunatic crying out for release from the evil spirits which were tormenting him, and saw the Gadarene swine go racing over the cliff. We noticed how the sheep and goats were separated, how women gathered round wells to draw water as precious as truth, how thorns grew in sand shining like precious jewels in a crown, how the light of the setting sun beats down on a mountain peak to make a Transfiguration.

Not one single detail seemed to be missing. There was the road to Jericho along which the Good Samaritan passed, and Bethany where Mary and Martha lived, and the Mount of Olives with its view of Jerusalem – the city seen from there having about it some excruciating and yet entrancing poignancy, which makes Christ's famous cry from the heart all too comprehensible:

'O Jerusalem, Jerusalem, thou that killest the prophets, and stonest them which are sent unto thee, how often would I have gathered thy children together, even as a hen gathereth her chickens under her wings....'

It is even possible to take the road to Emmaus, as Cleopas and his companion did, thinking along the way like them about the events of the Crucifixion – two thousand years ago or yesterday – to the point that one becomes aware, as they did, of another presence detaching itself from the shadows and accompanying one along the dusty stony way.

+⊱—⊰+

20

THE GOSPEL OF JESUS ÉGALITÉ

It has always seemed to me obvious that any religious response to life, however primitive, conveys more about its true nature than any intellectual one, however sophisticated. On this basis, an animist bowing down before a painted stone is nearer to the ultimate reality of things than ever Newton was when the apple fell on his head; and any Buddhist monk at his prayerwheel outshines an Einstein or a Bertrand Russell when it comes to grasping and responding to our essential human predicament.

Thus, however sceptical my own state of mind might otherwise be, I have always had a great appreciation of worship, and of the sacred music, architecture and other embellishments that go therewith. My fellow-humans, likewise, have seemed to me at their most appealing when they are kneeling in prayer, or singing their creator's praises. Contrariwise, at their most repellent when, as the Prayer Book has it, they are following too much the devices and desires of their own hearts. For instance, anguishedly watching the little roulette ball settle, or staring randily at erotica, or engaging in demagogy, mouth cavernously opening and arms gesticulating, or obsequiously helping a putative patron on with his overcoat after listening with a fixed smirk to his tedious tales.

I used to love it in Cairo when the muezzin sounded (before it was taped), and the hawkers and hucksters all broke off to unfold their little mats, turn towards Mecca, and, summoning up an expression of humility and sweetness, began to intone their prayers. The moment they had finished, of course, they resumed their hawking and huckstering more stridently than ever, at the precise point they had broken off; but there had been an interlude. That's what worship is – an interlude.

Again, in French villages, those weird old crones in black, with their lined parchment faces, kneeling and mumbling and handling their rosaries before a candle-lit Madonna. Or, on a Sunday morning, families making their way to Mass; the bustling mother with wisps of lace about her head, the children self-consciously in their best clothes, the father washed and brushed and moving stiffly in durable black cloth, the bell insistently sounding to quicken their footsteps. So many and so diverse occasions – *mantras* heard across the muddy waters of the Ganges, plainsong sublimely filling the towering spaces of Chartres Cathedral, a Salvation Army band triumphant at a street corner, Rabbis assiduously wailing at their Wall – but always, in every case, a sense of pride being broken, of flesh humbled as knees are bent or a forehead is lowered into the dust, of brotherhood and equality realized in worship rather than fraudulently asserted in a polling-booth. Always that little clearing made in the dark jungle of the human will.

Today, it must be admitted, worship in any traditional shape or style is out of fashion; churches and chapels and temples and mosques are alike emptying, and the priestly function has largely passed to mind-mending psychiatrists, body-mending doctors, and society-mending ideologues and miscellaneous *enragés*. Indeed, worship itself has in many instances taken a leaf out of the books of these latter-day priests, producing a bizarre amalgam of their jargon and the noises of contemporary entertainment. The aspiring worshipper is all too often offered the melancholy alternatives of muted matins or evensong in the company of the tiny residue of the faithful, and what amounts to Jesus-orientated discotheques.

In this modernizing process, whether in the most august Roman Catholic congregations or the most wayward and obscure of Little Bethels, the same principle would seem to be at work – to make worship as like as possible to everyday life, in its language, its exhortations, its music and its petitions. Whereas the great cathedrals and other monuments to Christendom's two thousand years were designed to express the awe and wonder and joy of men audaciously reaching up to God, and the corresponding thankfulness that God should have deigned to become incarnate and reach down to them, the present tendency is, as it were, to look God straight in the eye and address him accordingly. It is as though the sansculottes had taken over in Heaven, deposing God the father, transforming the Son into a Jesus *Égalité*. and incorporating the Holy Ghost in twanged electronic pieties.

How amazed an Anthony Trollope would be today at what passes for worship in many an ancient Anglican edifice! No more 'Dearly beloved brethren, I pray and beseech you, as many as are here present . . .' Rather, God is urged to redress the terms of trade in favour of the underdeveloped countries, or to ensure that the Security Council comes out strongly in favour of majority rule in Rhodesia. At an evening service I attended recently a moon-faced young cleric with luxuriant mutton-chop whiskers prayed that we all might be made 'thinkers like Karl Marx', adding presumably to obviate any possibility of being misunderstood on high, 'some of whose ideas are good and some bad'. I entered a private reservation to contract out of this request, having no particular fancy to be a thinker, least of all one like Karl Marx.

Such petitions, as it seems to me, imply a naïvely partisan attitude scarcely becoming in a deity who has for aeons past been watching over the affairs of the universe He created. While it is perfectly comprehensible that there should be more joy in Heaven over one repentant sinner than over all the hosts of the just, who will seriously suppose that similar rejoicings attend, say, the replacement in a newly constituted African State of a white authoritarian regime by a black one? Only, perhaps, the World Council of Churches, that *ponsasinorum* of all Christian endeavour. For myself, I much prefer the style of the Book of Common Prayer, whose requests to God are carefully related to the frailties of our human disposition and uncertainties of our mortal circumstances. Witness, the delightful prayer of St Chrysostum, which asks that our desires and petitions may be fulfilled, but only 'as may be most expedient for us'.

Then there are the new translations of the Bible, each more flat-footed and banal than the last, from which the lessons are usually read. Who in his senses can prefer – choosing at random from innumerable examples – *Those who live on the level of our lower nature have their outlook formed by it, and that spells death; but those who live on the level of the spirit have the spiritual*

211

outlook, and that is life and peace, to the Authorised Version's *For to be carnally minded is death; but to be spiritually minded is life and peace?* Yet so it is among the great majority of clergy today. The reason they adduce for their strange preference is that the meaning is clearer, forgetting that in too ardent a quest for meaning the first casualty is liable to be truth. My own baptism of fire in this matter came when I was editor of *Punch*. Readers quite often wrote in to ask what a particular joke meant, and in attempting to explain it I invariably found that I drained it of whatever humour it possessed, to the point that recipients of my explanation would write back to tell me how now they understood the joke, but it didn't make them laugh. Laughter and mystical ecstasy are two twin heights (hence the gargoyles on cathedrals) to which the human spirit may aspire; they can be climbed but not explored, still less surveyed for building sites.

It is in the sermon, naturally, that the full force of modernization is felt. A trendy preacher commonly begins by denouncing his congregation as a lot of structured prigs who suppose that coming to church makes them morally superior to their fellows outside, whereas, in point of fact, any pimp, prostitute or criminal is nearer to Christ than they are. Thus lambasted, I find myself reflecting that, though I cannot claim to have been on more than nodding terms with any pimps, I have in the course of a mis-spent life been acquainted with a certain number of prostitutes and criminals. Neither category, in my experience, live up to the claims so often made for them from the pulpit, the former being sluttish, lazy and self-indulgent, and the latter intolerably conceited, arrogant and self-centred. To insist that the founder of the Christian religion had a special affinity with them would seem to me as preposterous as suggesting that Quaker pacifists are never more at home than among Bornean head-hunters, or vegetarians at a dinner of the Worshipful Company of Butchers. Christ came into the world to save sinners, certainly, but not to exalt them; he was merciful to the woman taken in adultery, and exposed the hypocrisy of her accusers, but his last word to her - usually, by the way, omitted in permissive celebrations of this episode - was to go away and sin no more.

After his initial assault on the congregation, our preacher more often than not proceeds to confound them with denunciations of the church, its doctrines, its liturgy and history, its snivelling hymns and grovelling prayers, its derisory Thirty-Nine Articles, its very ornaments and missals, which, he thunders, would be far better sold and the proceeds given to the poor. I once heard a Dean carrying on like this in his own cathedral, and ending up with an appeal for funds to complete some structural alterations which had been put in hand. By this time we were all too battered and broken to make the obvious retort, and meekly contributed our mites; like mariners responding to an appeal from the captain for money to repair their ship just after he had announced his intention of running it onto the rocks. In the light of these and many other buffooneries, it must be considered little short of miraculous that Christian worship continues to attract any congregation at all. As Hilaire Belloc once remarked of his church, it had obviously enjoyed God's special favour and protection; otherwise, in view of the inane and often mischievous hands controlling its destiny, it would long since have disappeared.

In this connection, I recall an experience some years ago when I had occasion to pass several hours at Chicago Airport waiting for a plane connexion. Looking round desperately for an escape from the appalling noise, to my surprise I found, among the various amenities offered, a signpost pointing to a chapel. This proved to be a small twilit room with a Bible opened on a podium and a few rows of chairs. I settled down thankfully in one of these, only to find that even here the loud-speaker system operated, so that any meditation one might attempt was interrupted every few moments by an announcement that flight number so-and-so was boarding at such a gate, and all aboard, please. It seemed like a perfect image of much contemporary worship.

21

━┿━

ON THE SIDE OF LIFE

The great public excitement over the acquittal of Dr Leonard Arthur at Leicester Crown Court of the attempted murder of a Downs Syndrome, or mongol baby, carried my mind back to 1938. For it was in that year that Dr Aleck Bourne, a senior obstetrician, decided that it was his duty to perform an abortion on a 14-year-old girl who had been raped by several guardsmen. He duly carried out the operation, was tried, and like Dr Arthur, acquitted, to the accompaniment of considerable acclaim. Few, if any, of those who applauded him will have envisaged his acquittal making straight the way to abortion on demand some years later. This, however, was what happened, and Dr Bourne, observing it happen, came to regret his action; became, indeed, in due course, an ardent anti-abortionist.

How easily a compassionate impulse can thus be translated into a holocaust is well illustrated by the manner in which the acceptance in the Weimar Republic of euthanasia as enlightened and estimable, provided the initial justification in Hitler's Third Reich for the genocide programme of 1941-45. 'Technical experience gained first with killing psychiatric

215

patients,' Fredrick Wertham, writes in his deeply disturbing book, A Sign For Cain, 'was utilised later for the destruction of millions. The psychiatric murders came first.' While pictures of the Nazi holocaust were horrifying television and cinema audiences throughout the western world, all unbeknownst to them another ostensibly humane holocaust was being mounted, no less terrible than the other, for being aimed at enhancing the quality of life.

It requires no great prophetic power to foresee that the trial and acquittal of Dr Arthur may likewise be expected to prepare the way for acceptance of euthanasia as part of our contemporary way of life. At first, it will be a matter of disposing of seriously handicapped children who, for whatever reason, may be plausibly regarded as unlikely to appreciate the full quality of life available today – that is to say, to travel, drive a motorcar, have sex, watch television, and otherwise relish the devices and desires on offer in the twentieth century. We may assume, then, that soon there would be no more mongol children needing special care at home or institutions. Materialistically considered, this would be a solid gain; the quality of human livestock will be to that extent improved.

Some mothers, it is true, have found a special joy in caring for their mongol children. I am thinking, for instance, of Mary Craig who, in her splendidly honest book *Blessings*, describes how spiritually rewarding had been looking after her appallingly disturbed and distorted second child, Paul. 'The fear of Paul's being dragged off to an institution was the blackest one of all, however agonising it might be to look after him, I could not face the prospect of letting him go.' Then there is Fr Bidone, a priest of rare quality who looks after several institutions for mongol children. Occasionally, I have visited him, and always come away feeling happy and uplifted. Once he brought some of his boys to see me off at Heathrow Airport. At first, to my shame, I was a little embarrassed and then, looking around, I noticed that everyone, staff and passengers alike, was smiling. It seems as though God has put in these boys some special lovingness and joy in life to compensate for their deformity.

Nevertheless, in terms of the quality of life there would seem to be little reason for keeping such boys alive. If they are disposed of before or just after birth, those responsible for looking after them would be relieved of what can be a burdensome duty, and the boys themselves, of an existence that, in worldly terms, could never be other than unsatisfactory. The same reasoning applies to the infirm and senile old. Caring for them is expensive and exhausting; they themselves, as one sees them in old people's homes sitting around with nothing to do, would seem to be just waiting to die. In terms, however, of the sanctity of life the situation is quite different. Sanctity of life is a religious or transcendental concept, not a materialistic one, and presupposes the existence of a God, and a destiny for his creation reaching beyond the confines of time and mortality. All of us, the most learned, the ablest, the most charismatic, are equally infinitesimal in relation to our creator, and, seen across eternity, can scarcely be distinguished one from another.

How, then, can any decision be made that such a person should not be allowed to be born, and such another person not be allowed to go on living? That a mongol child has no right to be born or to live? Or that some mumbling old gaffer would be better dead? If life is sacred, it can only be wholly so; it cannot be sacred in parts; just as, if life is worth living at all, it can only be in all-conceivable and inconceivable circumstances. Its sacredness extends to every aspect of our existence, to whoever and whatever participates in the amazing creativity responsible for a measureless universe and a grain of sand, for elephants and fleas, for joy and woe.

It would seem to be a choice between these two – the quality of life and the sanctity of life. Which side are we on? On the one hand, keeping down our numbers so that we get ever more affluent – 2.5 kids at the most, controlling the new arrivals to ensure that they are top grade in mind and body, and the departures to ensure that they are eased out of this world as they begin to show signs of decrepitude. On the other hand, the sanctity of life, with mankind as a family whose father is God in whose image they are made; not equal but brothers, our families the microcosm of our creator's macrocosm. It would seem that the tide is flowing fast and furiously towards the former of these alternatives; I am for the latter, and confident that its ultimate triumph is certain.

22

‹∺═∺›

'FEED MY SHEEP'

An advantage of being, as I am, only a belated reader of the New Testament, is that one often finds a freshness of enchantment in sentences and phrases which, I imagine, come to seem commonplace to more erudite and systematic readers. This is what happened with the three words, 'Feed my sheep'. I found myself saying them over and over with a sense of great joyfulness, as though they were the key to some special revelation. One of those crystallizations of meaning which mystics and poets fashion for us. They occur, of course, in a rather curious thrice-repeated exchange between Peter and the risen Christ, in which, having asked Peter three times if he loved him, and being assured each time that he did, Jesus added, first, 'Feed my lambs,' and then, the other two times, 'Feed my sheep.' It irresistibly recalls that three-fold denial of his Master of which poor Peter has been guilty shortly before – something I can never recall without an agonizing pang at having likewise offended, not just once on a dramatic occasion, but again and again.

A shepherd and his flock provided Jesus with one of his favourite images. Even today in the Holy Land one can easily see why. The shepherd tending his sheep, finding them shade and water, seeing that none stray too far away, picking up in his arms one who may be lame or too small to keep up with the others, is still a familiar sight. It perfectly demonstrates in simply earthly terms Jesus' purpose in coming among us; he was the Good Shepherd, and so he has been known through the centuries. I find it rather sad to reflect that this imagery is soon to become obsolete and incomprehensible in our technological world, if it hasn't become so already.

One can scarcely look for the Good Shepherd in factory farms, where animals are accorded just enough statutory room to stand up in; where they never see the light of the sun, or the green of the grass, or the blue of the sky. Still less in the manufacture of our food requirements from petroleum products and other such unappetizing substances. Who, I wonder, will be able to detect the image of a Saviour in the man with the hormone-injector, whose ministrations are liable to transform our domestic animals into weird, unseemly, top-heavy creatures, mercifully hidden from view?

Surely, the first necessity we are under is to respect life; every aspect of it. Not just those of our fellow men who are dear and familiar to us, our families and friends. Nor even just our fellow humans who share the same essential experience of living. All and every manifestation of life; the croak of a frog, the contour of a hill, even the very particles of desert dust and the obscure flowering of hidden verges. All that lives and is on our small earth and in the illimitable universe. So 'Feed my sheep' applies to the whole flock, black, white and piebald. There are no exceptions. If we fail in according this respect to life as such, if in our insensate greed we wreck and impoverish and poison our human habitation, then we may be sure that in the long run we shall wreck and impoverish and poison ourselves.

We live in a society which can produce in more or less unlimited quantities everything, and more than everything, we can possibly want to feed and clothe and divert ourselves. From turbines to potato crisps, from giant airliners to birth pills – everything. The problem with us is not food supplies, but appetite. How to induce us to eat when we're not hungry, to discard what is not worn out, to indulge every whim and fancy that vanity and the senses can be lured into entertaining. So appeals to cupidity, appeals to sensuality, appeals to morbidity, all on behalf of the great Moloch – Consumption. The same message spelt out in neon lights, printed in words, embellished in colour, yelled in discotheques, whispered by crooners, related to the built-in urges of our way of life – money, sex and violence. An enormous flourishing industry, designed to ensure that greed never flags, sensuality never abates; that our heart's desire is caught for ever in traps that are fastened to the earth and baited with flesh.

Then the other side of the picture. Calcutta in the early morning; the streets strewn with the sleeping destitute and homeless, the garbage piled high and a few early risers poking about in it for something edible. A macabre fantasy, a tiny corner of a vast and mounting tragedy involving the greater part of the human race.

Confronted with this crazy contradiction between, on the one hand, so many hungry sheep, and, on the other, so many over-indulged ones under constant pressure and persuasion to indulge themselves further, what is to be done? There are those who very properly attempt to rectify the balance by charitable endeavour or political agitation. Others, particularly among the young, consider that the only valid answer is yet another revolution whereby, as is promised in the 'Magnificat', the hungry will be filled with good things and the rich sent empty away. A more self-righteous approach to the problem lies in attributing the trouble to there being too many people in the world. When I was young the same sort of attitude was taken by the middle and upper classes towards the poor. They had selfishly become too numerous, they were told. So today, when the so-called developing nations ask for bread, we give them birth pills. Has there ever, I wonder, been a stranger evangel than this - missionaries of sterility, colporteurs of contraceptives; bearers, as though it were our civilisation's proudest product, of ingeniously devised means to make procreation unprocreative? 'Feed my sheep,' yes, but not, surely, with birth pills!

Jesus himself well understood what poverty is from first-hand experience. He lived for the most part among the poor, and, as the Gospels tell us, unlike foxes which have holes and the birds of the air which have nests, often had nowhere to lay his head. Through the centuries that followed some of the most attractive and effective of his followers, from St Francis to Mother Teresa, have sought and loved poverty for his sake. Jesus also knew what riches were and what they do to people. In the Roman cities of Tiberias and Capernaum, whose ruins one may see today by the Lake of Galilee, he could observe a way of life uncommonly like ours, an affluent, permissive society dedicated to growing ever more affluent and permissive, with the games providing, like our media, the vicarious and morally debilitating excitement of violence and eroticism.

When Jesus said 'Feed my sheep' he was not, then, launching a charitable appeal, or proclaiming a revolution, or even preparing the way for a family-planning service. He himself, he said, was the bread of life, and no one partaking of it would ever again hunger or thirst. In 20th-century terms this seems like expressing indifference to actual physical hunger and deprivation, but quite the opposite was the case. Through the life and teaching of Jesus we may know how the suffering of every living creature, even of a sparrow falling to the ground, is part of the suffering of God, and that his purpose for us comprises seeking in all circumstances to relieve suffering and to help and support the weak and the oppressed. How to put into words this innermost mystery of the Christian Faith? That it is only in being indifferent to our bodily needs that we can truly care about them in others. That it is only in seeing beyond this world that we can truly see into its troubles and its beauties, and only in being a stranger here on earth and among our fellow men that the earth can be so dear a home and mankind so dear a family. That to live we must die.

It was accompanying Mother Teresa in Calcutta to the scene of the various activities of her Missionaries of Charity, to the house of the dying where derelicts from the streets are brought in so that at least in their last moments they may see a loving face and hear a word of love, to the homes for unwanted children sometimes pulled out of dustbins, and to the leper settlements, that I came nearest to understanding for a moment what Jesus meant by feeding his sheep. For I had reached beyond horror and beyond compassion, into an awareness never before experienced that somehow these dying and derelict human beings, these abandoned children and lepers with stumps instead of arms, were not repulsive or pitiable, but brothers and sisters upon whom, through the agency of Mother Teresa's perfect dedication, the bright radiance of God's universal love shone, as it does on all creation.

23

FINDING FAITH

A year has gone by since my wife Kitty and I were received into the Catholic Church. It has been, for us, a
year of happiness and inner serenity. Something of great importance has been finally settled for us; like Pascal we might
have cried out: 'Certainty, Certainty, Certainty, joy, peace, God
of Jesus Christ, Thy God should be my God, oblivion of the
world and of everything except God'. Thus the doubts that
we have entertained and even cherished during the years of
my life, all melt away or change their tenor, like reinforced
concrete, strengthening rather than weakening the faith they
seemed to jeopardise.

St. Paul's famous definition of faith: – 'the substance of
things hoped for, the evidence of things not seen', seems to
me perfect. Surely it is the gift most to be desired on earth.
The greatest minds have realised all too clearly the limitations
of the intellect as a means of exploring what life is about, just
because they have marched so far and so audaciously along
that particular road.

The situation is well expressed in one of my favourite books
– 'The Cloud of Unknowing', supposedly written by a monk

in the 14th century. 'For one thing I tell thee,' he writes, 'that there was never yet pure creatures in this life, nor yet shall be, so high ravished in contemplation of the Godhead that there is not evermore a wonderful Cloud of Unknowing twixt him and his God'. Of God himself, he goes on, 'Can no man think.....He may be loved but not thought. By love he may be gotten and holden, but by thought never'. It is a beautiful image and we of the 20th century have every reason to be well aware of the appalling consequences of its obverse, a Cloud of Knowing which generates pride and fantasy to the point of bringing into range the possibility of blowing ourselves and our little earth to smithereens.

'If the sun and moon should doubt,' Blake wrote, 'they'd immediately go out.' Without faith, that is to say, there is only night, however brightly the neon lights may shine, however fast the jet planes fly, and however glamorous the coloured pictures glow. There is, it seems to me, no substitute for faith. Without it, life is unliveable. It is the sense that faith gives of a universal spiritual order that alone makes it possible to establish some sort of temporal, moral, social or political order. Without the one, as we are now dramatically seeing, the other breaks down. As faith disappears chaos becomes inevitable; as its light goes out darkness must fall.

It has been a great comfort to know that one is a member of a Church whose leadership at any rate is unequivocally opposed to legalised abortion and other aspects of the appalling, ostensibly humane, holocaust which turns hospitals into abattoirs wherein unborn children and the ailing old are systematically murdered. For myself the great boon and blessing of the Church is that it enshrines not a panacea for contemporary ills, or the promise of future happiness, but a mystery – that all creation, its totality, is one; the manifestation of a loving creator whose reach is between the furthermost limits of the universe and the counted hairs of each individual human head – who, as George Herbert so exquisitely puts it, 'dost stretch a crumme of dust from heaven to hell.'

Faith tells me it is possible to establish with this loving creator a living and loving relationship which makes all things joyously comprehensible and acceptable. It also tells me that through the Christian revelation our relationship with our creator is translated into human terms. God became a man, a man became God, in order that we might know God, not just as a notion, but as a father in heaven whose family we all are.

Christ's death on the Cross, and His subsequent living presence in the world, provides the bridge between mortality and immortality, between man and his creator and between time and eternity.

24

＋＞━━＜＋

TIME AND ETERNITY

People speak of wasting time, but in fact it's the other way round. Time wastes us. I always seem to hear clocks ticking, even when there are no clocks - as in the middle of Australia, or in Berlin's liberated rubble which looked as timeless as the mountains of the Moon. We are born into time, and, living, it enfolds us inescapably. Time is, for us, a prison, and eternity the light we peer at through the bars. Time is something which inexorably ends, as today does, and tomorrow, and this year, and this century, and the earth itself, and the universe. Everything ends except eternity, which cannot end because it never began.

Time ticks on from minute to minute and hour to hour, without ever adding up to eternity. *Ah! sunflower! weary of time who countest the steps of the sun.* I, too, have counted them, to the point of weariness, and then lost count. The steps of the sun go up to eternity, but we who climb them so assiduously and eagerly never get any nearer to the top. *I saw eternity the other night, like a great ring of pure and endless light, all calm as it was bright; and round beneath it, time in hours, days, years, driven by the spheres like a vast shadow moved.* Eternity can be thus seen, but we *live* in time. It is our habitat; as fishes live in water and birds in air, we live in time.

Yet we carefully detach from time everything we admire or want to be. Heaven, we say, lies beyond time; love is not just for today or tomorrow, but for eternity; great works of art and great truths are eternal, as are all deities, whether anthropomorphic or transcendental. Time is as paltry as *Time* magazine. Even contemporary advocates of drugs like mescaline and LSD claim for them that they take their users out of time, thereby recognising that this is a desirable situation. Though time governs us we look askance at it; though eternity is outside our experience and beyond our comprehension, we pine for it with sick longing. We vote for eternity in our dreams even though we draw our cheques on time when we are awake. Killing time! - what a marvellous expression! It's precisely what we do all the while - getting rid of it like garden rubbish by slow or quick combustion.

But at my back I always hear time's winged chariot hurrying near, and yonder all before us lie deserts of vast eternity. It's on these deserts that our eyes are irretrievably fixed. How strange, I often reflect, that the bodies we nurture so zealously, the appetites we cultivate so assiduously, the wealth or fame or power we seek so ardently, all belong to time which we despise, and their negation to eternity, the focus of all our hopes and desires.

Whatever we do is temporal, whatever we aspire after is eternal. Deeds belong to time, ideas to eternity. The hand which writes these words belongs to a body soon to expire; the mind which thinks them will likewise in a decade or so at most function no more. Both belong to time, and like all time's creatures are mortal. Yet the words themselves, however banal, inadequate and inconsequential, however transient their impact on other minds, are projected like satellites into the empty space of eternity, there to orbit.

Such is our human situation. We live on an eternal shore against which time's breakers endlessly pound. Ascetics have tried to escape altogether from time, sensualists to bury themselves in it. Neither can succeed. I return to my earlier image. Serving our mortal sentence (in the most literal sense, doing time) we look out through the prison bars at eternity, looking forward to the day when the great gates of time will open and we shall be released.

Notes

Malcolm Muggeridge's papers are deposited at the Buswell Memorial Library Special Collections, Wheaton College, Illinois, USA. The abbreviations UMWC and MWC refer respectively to undated and dated manuscripts now at Wheaton College. Any approximate dates are based on similar works and biographical details. When Muggeridge was preparing his collection of essays, *Tread Softly lest you Tread on my Jokes* (1966), in a few instances he ran two pieces together to read as one. I have followed him in this in *The Kingdom of Heaven on Earth, Eight Books, Heroes of their Time, Two Writers* and *Finding Faith*. These and any other significant adjustments are recorded in the following notes. My sole criteria throughout, was to present these wonderful works to the reader as Malcolm might have edited them himself. Original titles in the Notes are italicised. Muggeridge often wrote or typed out the first draft without undue reference to paragraphing, which he would sometimes indicate when doing corrections. When this was not done, or when a newspaper layout has seemed to impose an illogical spacing, I have adjusted the paragraphs without comment, as I have any occasional misprint or obvious error.

1. The Collectivisation of the Ukraine *The Soviet and the Peasantry: an Observer's Notes*. Manchester Guardian (26, 27 and 28 March 1933). 'The novelty of this particular famine, what made it so diabolical, is that it was not the result of some

catastrophe like a drought or an epidemic. It was the deliberate creation of a bureaucratic mind which demanded the collectivisation of agriculture, immediately, as a purely theoretical proposition, without any consideration whatever of the consequences in human suffering . . . the famine is the most terrible thing I have ever seen, precisely because of the deliberation with which it was done and the total absence of any sympathy with the people.' Malcolm Muggeridge (19 Feb 1983).

2. The Soul of Bolshevism. Condensed from *Russia Revealed*. Morning Post (5, 6, 7 and 8 June 1933}.

3. The Kingdom of Heaven on Earth. Extracted from *The Kingdom of Heaven on Earth*. New English Review (May 1949) and Men and Books, a review of F.A. Voight's *Unto Ceasar*. Time and Tide (9 April 1938).

4. Nazi Terror. *What Government by Terror Means*. Observer (9 Dec 1939).

5. The Phoney War. UMWC (1949?). This extract is taken from the first draft of an unfinished book *The Forties*. I have omitted the extensive footnotes, some of which Muggeridge may have intended either to discard or to incorporate into the text of a later draft. This manuscript was discovered at a publisher's 45 years after it was written, and arrived at Wheaton College during the ten days I spent there in 1995. That coincidence was enough to convince me that part of it ought to be used.

6. Letters from America. MWC (1946/47). Letters written to Kitty Muggeridge while Malcolm was Washington correspondent for the Daily Telegraph.

7. Fellow Travellers. *Wither are all the Fellow Travellers Going?* Daily Telegraph (29 July 1948).

8. Heroes of Their Time: Bertrand Russell and D.H. Lawrence.

The New Republic (3 April 1976) Esquire (April 1968)

Muggeridge was an admirer of Mikhail Lermontov's novel: *A Hero of Our Time,* in which the author wrote, in his foreword, that it was, ' indeed a portrait, but not of one man; [but] a portrait built up of all our generation's vices in full bloom.' Lermontov's title is adapted here for these pithy, and critical, assessments of two influential twentieth century thinkers.

9. *Dayspring from on High.* UMWC (1949?). In editing this unfinished essay – clearly still in its early stages – I have not tried to impose a cohesion or sequence of thought that is not in the original text. Rather, I saw it as being similar in form to Pascal's Pensées. The parts left out are those that are repetitive (in this draft Muggeridge allowed his ideas to flow onto the page without reference to previous passages), or those in which the ideas expressed are found elsewhere in his work. Even in its unfinished state it gives a fascinating insight into Muggeridge's inner spiritual life.

10. *The Prophet of Sex.* New Statesman (12 May 1967).

11. Two Writers: Somerset Maugham and Leonard Woolf.

Observer (11 Dec 1965). Observer (17 Aug 1969). In both of these portraits, the writers appear, somehow bereft and forlorn, due perhaps to the lack of any religious belief, thereby throwing emphasis on the succeeding essays.

12. Eight Books. *Life with Picasso* by Françoise Gilot and Carlton Lake. Esquire (March 1965). Edmund Wilson *The Dead Sea Scrolls, 1947-1969. Esquire (19690.* Jason Epstein *The Great Conspiracy Trial* and Tom Haydon *Trial.* Esquire (1971). George L Jackson *Blood in my Eye.* Esquire (1972). John Passmore The *Perfectibility of Man.* Observer (17 July 1970). Sylvia Press *The Care of Devils.* Esquire (May 1966). Henri Charrière Papillon. Observer (17 April 1970).

13. In The Beginning was the word. *Le Mot Injuste.* UMWC (1970s?).

14. *Lie in the Camera's Eye.* The Times (1st April 1972)

15. *Russia Revisited. Behind the cruel propositions the ancient greeting.* The Guardian (11 April 1983).

16. *Solzhenitsyn Reconsidered.* The American Spectator (Dec 1980).

17. The Law of Love and Law of Violence. *Tolstoy's Valedictory.* Observer (25 Jan 1970). The articles that come after this slightly shortened tribute to Tolstoy, and the following letters could be said – in the context of this book – to state Muggeridge's own Valedictory.

18. Letters to Kitty. MWC. Written to Kitty Muggeridge (1962/69). In *Jesus Rediscovered,* Muggeridge mentions 'someone infinitely dear' to him, who 'had gone temporarily mad'. In these letters, he refers to his daughter Valentine and that experience. April 18, 67, written from Nunraw while filming the BBC film A Hard

Bed to Lie On Aug 2, 67, 'B' refers to Beatrice Webb, Kitty's aunt, about whom she wrote a biography with Ruth Adam. Oct 9, the 'Graham' mentioned is almost certainly Graham Greene, with whom Muggeridge had a long, though sometimes uneasy, friendship. April 30, 68, – April 5, 69, 'Hughie' – Hugh Kingsmill (1889–1949).

19. The Holy Land. *Thoughts in the Holy Land*. Observer (24 Dec 1967).

20. *The Gospel of Jesus Egalité*. Times Saturday Review (2 Sept 1972).

21. *On the Side of Life*. Sunday Times (10 Nov 1981). Dr. Leonard Arthur was tried at the Leicester Crown Court in Oct/Nov 1981 before Mr. Justice Farquharson, for the murder of John Pearson, a newly born Down's syndrome baby. Dr. Arthur prescribed 'nursing care only' for John Pearson, who was born 28 June 1980 and died 5 Feb 1981. 'Nursing care only' in this instance was a euphemism for starvation and the administration of DF118, a drug meant to be given with food, and unsuitable for children under four years old ('the blood level of the drug actually found in the baby's body was more than twice the amount sufficient to kill an adult.' *Life*). After initially stating these details, the Judge subsequently referred to the administration of DF118 and water as 'feeds'. Dr. Arthur was acquitted.

22. 'Feed my Sheep'. From *What Christ meant when he said Feed my Sheep*. New Zealand Tablet (17 Jan 1973).

23. Finding Faith. Adapted from *What is Faith?* Catholic Herald (21 June 1968) and *My first year as a Catholic*. Universe (25 Nov 1983)

24. *Time and Eternity*. UMWC (1980s?).

25. Notes.

26. Acknowledgements.

Acknowledgements

First and foremost, I would like to acknowledge my gratitude and amazement, at my wife Judy's loving, unwavering, and unselfish support for this project, at my four daughters, Carrie, Sonia, Teresa and Monica's sustained belief in 'the Muggeridge book' through the wilderness years, and at the providential route that led me to Sally Bolt of David Bolt Associates, who turned my dream into reality. I am also immensely grateful to Brendan Walsh and his colleagues at Darton, Longman and Todd for taking *Time and Eternity* in out of the cold and giving it such a good home.

Looking back I can honestly say, echoing the words of Isabella Beeton on completing her book on household management, that if I had known at the outset the labour this book would cause me, I never would have had the courage to undertake it. However the task was only made possible with the help of numerous individuals, some of who are among the following:

The late Valentine Colenbrander, the late John Muggeridge and Leonard Muggeridge, for giving me permission to study their father's papers and reproduce them in this book.

(Quotations from other works that are included in the main body of the book, by in large, formed part of reviews and are reproduced in that context. Quotations in the introduction and the words prefixing it by Simone Weil, are used with permission).

The Quotation from one of Han Shan's Cold Mountain Poems, translated by Burton Watson, quoted in my introduction is used by permission of Columbia University Press.

The staff at the Buswell Memorial Library Special Collections, Wheaton College, Illinois, for all their help – what a great place!

The staff at the Colindale library, London.

Myrna Grant, who put me up on my first night in Chicago.

Mary Anne and William Phemister, who showed me great kindness when I lodged with them at Wheaton.

The late Isaac Guillory, who asked his cousin Joseph Bleckman (who did not know me) to meet me at the airport on my arrival in America and show me round – something he did in great style, nearly getting me killed on my first day in Chicago. I'm happy to say that Joseph and I became great friends and remain so.

Richard Ingrams, who read an early draft of the manuscript and made a valuable suggestion, which I adopted.

My daughter Teresa Mills, who went well beyond the call of duty when I was having computer problems, becoming my indefatigable ally in a thousand and one ways – thanks Mush!

My brother James, who was always willing to be a sounding-board for my not always sound ideas and who gave me much valuable advice.

Sally Muggeridge and David Williams of The Malcolm Muggeridge Society for their support and assistance.

Jeff Mowatt and Howard Lane, for incalculable help with computer problems and photocopying.

And last but not least, Jim of the Wheaton Bar, for cigarettes when I ran out and cool beers in the Chicago heat wave of

95. You said; 'I hope you'll speak well of us all when you go back to England'. And I always have, and will.